4.95

THE BIG BANG

The Financial Revolution in the City of London and What it Means for You

THE BIG BANG

The Financial Revolution in the City of London and What it Means for You

Guy Galletly & Nicholas Ritchie

Northcote House

Galletly, Guy
The big bang: the financial revolution in the City of London and what it means for you.
1. Financial institutions — England — London
2. Financial institutions — Law and legislation — England — London
I. Title II. Galletly, Guy
332.1'09421' HG186.G7

Acknowledgements
The Authors wish to express their gratitude to the following for supplying photographs: The Bank of England, Lloyd's of London, Lloyds Bank Plc, London International Financial Futures Exchange, and The Stock Exchange, London; and to Methuen Children's Books for permission to use the quotation from A. A. Milne's *Winnie-The-Pooh*.

First published in 1986 by Northcote House Publishers Ltd,
Harper & Row House, Estover Road, Plymouth PL6 7PZ,
United Kingdom. Tel: Plymouth (0752) 705251. Telex 45635.

Printed and bound in Great Britain by Tamar Print Ltd.

Contents

Part One
Why We Are Where We Are

1
Introduction

'BANG !!!???***!!!
Piglet lay there, wondering what had happened. At first he thought that the whole world had blown up; and then he thought that perhaps only the Forest part of it had; and then he thought that perhaps only *he* had . . .' From *Winnie-the-Pooh* by A. A. Milne.

The Big Bang: What It Isn't . . .

With all the talk of a Big Bang, many people will doubtless be wondering, like Piglet, exactly *who* or *what* has blown up? Some knowledgeable persons, of course, are quite *au fait* with such things. They have long since familiarised themselves with theories of how the world began and taken up their intellectual stand either at the pole of 'steady state' or its opposite. For them, further reading is unnecessary: it would merely cloud the issues.

Others, having a relish for the cataclysmic, know that the Big Bang really refers to the inevitable nuclear holocaust towards which the world is hurtling heedless and headlong, and of which Chernobyl is merely a bitter foretaste. That will be the Big Bang to end all Big Bangs, of course, so for them too further reading is pointless. All that remains is to eat, drink and be merry.

. . . And What It Is:

But eating, drinking and being merry cost money, earned by trading goods and services with other people. It will not be long, therefore, before everyone in our society becomes aware of the third Big Bang. Like the other two already mentioned, it will certainly affect us all. The post Big Bang world will be different: financial systems will behave differently. But, happily, no one will be atomised in the process and, indeed, many people should in fact be better off and more financially secure as a result.

The Big Bang has come to mean the series of changes initiated by an agreement between the government and the London Stock Exchange in

1983. Under this agreement, the Stock Exchange abandoned certain rules which had restricted competition; in return it was exempted from prosecution under the Restrictive Practices laws. The term 'Big Bang' was originally used, however, to describe the arrangements for implementing this agreement, which was to be done on a specified date three years later, rather than piecemeal over the intervening period of time.

The official date of this Big Bang is 27th October 1986. It will happen in 'the City' — an area in London where most British financial institutions have their head offices and also the nerve centre of the UK's whole financial system. In reality, not all the changes associated with the Big Bang will take place on that one day. Much has already been done, and the consequences will work themselves out far into the future. The significance of 27th October is that on that date, the keystone of the arch which is central to the whole financial edifice will be set in place when the new Stock Exchange rule book comes into full effect. It is a target date, set three years before, to give focus and form to the timetable of changes taking place at the Stock Exchange.

The City

Historically, the City of London derived its pre-eminence from its superb geographical position; as a seaport facing the Continent it had ready access to the trading routes of the world. Many of today's great City institutions have their origins in ocean-going trade. For example, Lloyd's Insurance Corporation grew out of a coffee house near the docks operated by Edward Lloyd for the convenience of merchants who met there to do business. Gradually, almost every conceivable aspect of trade, whether in physical commodities or in financial assets, has opened a market place or exchange somewhere within the Square Mile between St. Paul's in the west and the Tower of London in the east. The process still continues. New markets are being established every decade to meet new needs; witness the London International Financial Futures market opened in the Royal Exchange in 1982.

The political and military power achieved by Great Britain since the seventeenth century conferred upon the City of London a great deal of prestige and prosperity. It became the financial centre of the world, a magnet for funds and financial acumen which, in turn, encouraged further innovation in a virtuous spiral — one which is still operating as we near the end of the twentieth century. In market after market, the City is either the outright world leader or at least among the top three. It is an impressive record for a small country.

Lloyds Bank computer control room: the nerve centre of a big bank.

However, this virtuous spiral had very nearly ceased to operate on account of the growth of a wide range of rigidities and obstructions in the system. Other countries, particularly the United States, were surging forward without these chains. As a result, the City's share of markets had been slipping. The Big Bang revolution is thus essentially about breaking free of out-of-date restrictions, about modernising and streamlining and adapting institutions to the needs and opportunities of our times.

Unfortunately, revolution is one of those words whose meaning has become watered down by excessive and inappropriate use. But, in this case, no other word would be adequate to describe the speed and scale of the changes taking place in the City today. Daily procedures which have lasted for two generations are being swept away almost overnight. Like all revolutions, however, this one has its roots in the past, so by doing a little digging we can make more sense of the present.

Origins of the Big Bang

All revolutions tend to proceed in two stages. First there is a long period during which growing dissatisfaction with the old regime is kept in check by the authorities who use a variety of methods — some persuasive and some coercive — to suppress open manifestations of discontent. Their long term success in doing this depends on how well they can adapt their institutions and practices to the needs of the people most directly affected by them. A failure to adapt, linked to policies merely designed to suppress opposition, can only postpone problems — never remove them. The second stage is reached when some quite minor event, or a series of them, sets off a chain reaction which then sweeps away the old order.

Let us therefore look at the factors that have, over the past ten or fifteen years, built up such a pressure for reform and, in so doing, given the comparatively minor changes at the Stock Exchange such explosive repercussions. The rest of this Part is about these factors.

2
Currency Movements: Exchange Rates and Controls

The market for foreign exchange is much like any other market. The people who want to buy bring money to the market and those who want to sell bring their goods. The only difference in foreign exchange markets is that the 'goods' are one sort of currency — say pounds sterling — and the money is another — say dollars. However, the fundamental laws of economics which say that, when goods are in short supply their price will go up, still hold. When pounds are scarce, their price in terms of dollars will appreciate — in free markets, at least.

The people who supply sterling to the market fall into two categories. First there are those who want to buy foreign imports, which leads to transactions on the current account of the balance of payments accounts; and second there are those who wish to buy foreign capital — capital account transactions.

In both cases, what is being bought has to be paid for in the local currency of the supplier. British buyers of foreign goods and capital, for example, have to convert their pounds to that foreign currency. Buyers of foreign assets include those who wish to buy long term fixed capital (factories in the US, for example) as well as those who want to buy shorter term financial assets (for instance, shares or bonds issued by American enterprises).

Similarly, the people who buy sterling on the foreign exchange market are foreigners who wish to buy British exports or capital. A large flow of sterling initiated by any of these groups separately, or in combination, will be enough to alter its price.

Governments also play a part in this market. The exchange rate will ultimately determine the price of UK exports and imports and so affect Britain's competitiveness overseas, as well as the domestic rate of inflation. Furthermore, widely fluctuating exchange rates create uncertainty and make the planning of business activity more difficult. Thus, if a French purchaser of an English machine tool cannot be sure of the price in francs that he will have to pay on delivery, he may not order it at all. Governments have therefore intervened in the market in a number of ways in order to get an exchange rate they believe to be both suitable and sustainable.

Governments were keen to do away with the volatile exchange rates of the inter-war period because they were felt to be responsible, in part, for the protectionist policies that led up to the second world war. Therefore, at the Bretton Woods conference in 1944 they worked out a system of fixed exchange rates for all major currencies. In practice, this meant that sterling and all other western currencies were pegged to a specific dollar price; this could only be changed in certain circumstances and after consulting the IMF.

This system worked admirably, so long as buyers and sellers of, say, sterling were content with the set price or 'parity'. If, however, a lot of people wished to sell pounds and dumped them on the market, their price would tend downwards. To keep it at the parity, the authorities had to redress the balance by buying up the surplus sterling with other currencies, to remove the downward pressure. Their ability to do this, of course, depended on the supply of other currencies at their disposal. When this ran out, and they could no longer intervene, then inevitably the price of the pound would fall or devalue.

By 1971, it was no longer possible to make the system work. Successive countries found that they had to devalue. Even the dollar itself came under strain and was finally devalued by the Smithsonian Agreement in December 1971. The solution adopted was that currencies began to float: that is, they were allowed to find their own level relative to each other without much government intervention. The oil price rises that followed soon afterwards put most of the western economies in deficit on the current accounts of their balance of payments, and this led to further exchange rate changes.

Western governments did not want the abolition of the fixed exchange rate system: it was forced upon them. Differences in inflation rates between countries, leading to differences in competitiveness, meant that some of them were running persistent balance of payments deficits. Their domestic policies, e.g. growth and full employment, prevented them from stemming these flows overseas; to do so would inevitably have led to stagnation and unemployment and other economic evils to which their electorate would naturally object. Governments therefore decided to bow to the inevitable and let their currencies float.

They did not, however, hand over total control of exchange rates to the market: they retained a battery of weapons with which to intervene should they feel the need. One of these weapons was exchange controls.

Although exchange controls were a wartime emergency measure, they were adopted permanently in 1947. Britain then was a near-bankrupt and exhausted economy trying to pick itself up after the second world war. The purpose of these controls was to restrict UK residents' purchases of foreign currency, and they effectively stopped individuals and institutions from exporting their savings. Balance of payments deficits were thus smaller than they might otherwise have been, and downward pressure on the value of the pound was eased. But, over the years, exchange control had the unlooked-for side-effect of allowing the British securities market to grow increasingly uncompetitive, cocooned from the ultimate discipline of its customers taking their money elsewhere.

The knock-on effect of this, as far as industry was concerned, was that it could obtain investment funds without offering the kind of rates of return that, say, American firms had to offer.

Abandonment of exchange controls in 1979 was, in part, an ideological decision by the Conservative government and, in part, an economic necessity. Conservatives are traditionally suspicious of the control of any market, feeling that if British entrepreneurs are free to invest wherever they wish they will choose wisely and profitably. Similarly, if the users of international funds are forced to pay the world market price, they will have to make only those investments that yield a competitive rate of return.

There were, however, other moves afoot which made the ending of exchange controls desirable, if not essential. By 1979, North Sea oil was coming on stream in a big way and the resulting balances on current account from the sale of the oil threatened to bid up the price of the pound to such an extent that UK manufactured and service exports would become very uncompetitive. It was therefore desirable to offset these current account inflows with a capital outflow. By giving up exchange controls, the government released the pent up demand of British financial institutions who had, for some time, wanted to diversify into foreign markets. Since then, some £30 billion has left Britain to buy securities abroad. And, correspondingly, British industry has been forced to improve its profitability or go to the wall for lack of investment.

There was a further consideration. It was becoming clear that many traditional UK manufacturing industries like cars, ships and engineering were losing market share to other countries. If, as seemed likely, they really were in long term decline, then it was important to ensure that some other industry grew up to make up their contribution to the balance of payments. As Britain has a comparative advantage in 'City' services, it seemed wise to encourage these, and the best way of doing so was to allow unfettered movement of foreign exchange both into and out of the UK. Depositors could then be confident when they sent their money to UK banks for investment that it would not get 'locked in'.

However, perhaps the most persuasive reason for dismantling exchange controls is that they are no longer capable of doing what they were designed to do — control the direction of investment and the value of the currency. The fact that western countries, including the UK, were unable to hold onto fixed currency parities, despite a whole battery of controls, shows the ineffectiveness of exchange controls. In practice, they were also almost as unsuccessful in keeping investment in the UK because they simply encouraged multinational corporations that earned profits overseas to keep them there.

It can be seen, then, that in the 1970s the exchange rate system and the accompanying regulations changed completely. This led to two key consequences with far-reaching results. First, the ending of fixed exchange rates meant that firms of all kinds were in danger of incurring exchange rate losses. If a bank held a stock of dollars and the dollar depreciated, it would obviously make a capital loss. Gains were possible as well. If a firm owed money in America and sterling appreciated, then it would need to spend less pounds to buy the dollars it needed to settle its debt. A whole industry sprang up dedicated to insulating traders from such losses, as did another dedicated to making speculative profits from the purchase and sale of foreign currency. It is now thought that the latter dominates the former in the foreign exchange market. Some writers suggest that as much as 95% of the money which passes through the market is speculative, and only the remaining 5% is in support of foreign trade.

Second, with the end of exchange control, London financial institutions were now free to compete world-wide with their counterparts; furthermore, foreign financial institutions now felt confident in opening branch offices or subsidiaries in London to compete directly for UK domestic business. This brought not only fresh competition but new techniques and attitudes. The gentleman's club atmosphere of the City was under threat from the players from overseas.

3
Interest Rates

Just as violently fluctuating exchange rates have brought about pressures for change in the City, so too have fluctuating interest rates.

Throughout the 1970s and since, governments have grappled with the problem of inflation using monetary measures; the effect of this has been to cause interest rates to move more rapidly and more unpredictably than ever before. This makes life difficult for businessmen who want to be certain of the interest cost of the investment they plan to make. Not surprisingly, they have tried to find ways of insulating themselves against unpredictable changes in interest rates — hence the need for a financial futures market which lets them hedge against such changes.

Firms have also been anxious to find ways of cutting their interest expense, and the whole panoply of new products devised by the investment banks has catered for this need. When interest rates are fairly stable and uniform, corporate treasurers tend to be passive and unenterprising. They like to do business with the bank they have always used. But when the market is fluid, and there is a variety of products to choose from, they tend to shop around. This requires a different, more market-oriented, sort of banking, and financial institutions must change accordingly.

4
Insensitive Regulation and Taxation

So far, we have seen how pressure for greater competitive freedom has come both from inside and outside the British financial system. The UK government, by its policies towards the management of the currency, has had a strong influence in promoting change. But any serious evaluation of the government's impact on the competitiveness of the financial sector must begin by taking account of the years of neglect during which successive governments have allowed practices to go on which would never have been tolerated in the industrial sector.

Besides turning a blind eye to uncompetitive practices in the City, post-war governments have enacted one fiscal measure after another without regard to the long term distortion caused to the patterns of demand and supply in the financial markets as a whole, and thus in the wider economy. For example, at times the banks have been stopped from raising interest rates to attract funds, while the building societies were left unrestricted. More money flowed into the societies and thus into home loans, and less remained to finance industry.

A large part of the fabulous wealth of the big financial institutions like insurance companies, pension funds and unit trusts, derives from past government policies which have favoured them. During the twenty years to 1984, according to Stockbrokers Phillips and Drew, private individuals' holdings of listed British shares fell from over half the total to under a quarter, while the big institutions increased theirs during the same period from 28% to 60% of the total.

No one can really tell what effect these fiscal measures have had with any precision. But it would be naive to believe that the high taxation of dividends and capital gains tax did not discourage private share ownership. Tax relief (now abolished) on life insurance premiums and pension contributions positively discriminated in favour of 'vicarious' shareholding by institutions adapted for the purpose. Unit trusts, for example, now run portfolios in excess of £14 billion, compared with £190 million only 25 years ago. Not even British inflation rates can account for growth on that scale.

High Taxes Have Been Bad For Business . . .

One big reason why these institutions have been keen to depart with their portfolios to foreign markets is to be found in the 2% stamp duty payable on share deals (halved to 1% in 1984). A fund manager who bought shares in London when he could just as easily buy the same shares on another exchange with less or no tax could hardly be said to be putting his clients' interests first, unless there were compensating advantages.

This led to the development of the market in ADRs (American Depository Receipts) which were created when large US securities houses bought huge blocks of shares in UK blue chip companies and paid the 2% stamp duty on the deal. All subsequent trading in these shares was then done in the US stock market where no duty was payable. As long as exchange restrictions were in force, this did not matter much to dealers in the UK domestic market. But since 1979, the effect of the stamp duty has simply been to force business away from the London Stock Exchange and therefore away from British brokers.

. . . But Arbitrary Tax Relief Has Been Harmful, Too

Another major bias in the UK's tax system, namely tax relief on mortgage interest, has also damaged the securities markets. Most obviously, it has sucked funds into bricks and mortar, starving other users of much-needed finance. More subtle, though, are the knock-on effects such as higher interest rates throughout the system and inexorably rising house prices. Firms wishing to borrow money to buy machinery — i.e. to undertake real investment — have had to pay more for it if they went to banks; and, even if they went direct to the securities markets, they also had to compete with the potential for capital gain which property offered.

Until recently, mortgage interest tax relief was given at the marginal rate of tax paid, so the richest individuals in terms of earned income (and hence the people most likely to buy shares) were especially encouraged to buy property instead.

Interestingly, this process may have come full circle: the earliest beneficiaries of the post-war property boom are now well into old age. When they die, they will, in many cases, leave hugely valuable houses which their children — themselves approaching middle age and already well housed — do not need. We may therefore expect some easing of the property market and a shift back towards other forms of asset holding — a move from which the securities market among others will benefit.

Not only has there been constant bias in the rates of tax levied, but also in the arrangements made to collect it. For years, the banks have been allowed to quote rates and pay interest on deposit accounts free of tax, leaving the depositor to account to the Inland Revenue in due course. This has made the banks' rates seem more attractive. Building societies, on the other hand, have long borne the burden of collecting, on the government's behalf, the tax on the interest earned by members' deposits. The societies, in their turn, gained some advantage from the fact that the actual rate of such tax paid by them was below the normal basic rate because it was a composite rate; it reflected the *average* tax rate of all the societies' depositors, many of whom should not be paying any tax at all, such as children and pensioners. The situation has now changed with the introduction, in 1985, of composite rate tax at source on bank deposit interest.

Competition Through Economic Necessity

Against such a background of uncoordinated competition and fiscal strategies, the present government's conversion to competition and deregulation in the City was not quite as natural as hindsight might make it appear. Mrs Thatcher's government believes in competition, certainly; but its monopolies and mergers policy has been ambiguous. It has not, for example, pressed ahead with the proposal to bring unions within competition legislation. What is more, it has presided over the greatest spurt of merger-mania since the 1960s, during which decisions about which deal should be referred to the Monopolies Commission, and which shouldn't, have been about as predictable as a roulette wheel.

The key to this enigma lies in the fact that the government did not think up City reform: it evolved largely through force of events. Like its predecessors, Mrs Thatcher's government has really stumbled on the City revolution more by accident than by design, primarily because of economic necessity which, as we saw, forced the abandonment first of fixed exchange rates and then of all other exchange controls.

5
Deregulation

The new Conservative government of 1979 asked itself why it was that, when London was the heart of the international insurance market and of international bank lending, its security markets lagged behind? The conclusion it came to was that the market structure was wrong; one that more closely resembled the eurocurrency markets (where there is no rule book whatever) was more likely to bring about success. Deregulation (i.e. the removal or reduction of rules) thus became the order of the day.

For a while, though, nothing much seemed to happen in the public domain. Then, very slowly, the government began to do away with some of the tax distortions. Out went life insurance premium tax relief; down came stamp duty; and in came composite rate tax on bank interest. Behind the scenes, however, a good deal more was going on. The Director General of Fair Trading and the Council of the Stock Exchange were locked in protracted negotiations over the Exchange's Rule Book which contained various provisions restricting Members' freedom in the conduct of their business.

The two main restrictive provisions were fixed minimum commissions (established in 1912) and single capacity trading (established in 1908). Fixed minimum commissions meant that the percentage brokers charged for their services was the same, regardless of the size of the transaction. Single capacity trading meant that two distinct classes of Member were created: brokers and jobbers. Brokers act on behalf of their clients, the general public and institutions, trading shares with the jobbers who deal on their own behalf. The jobbers' function was to act as wholesalers, making sure there was always a buyer or seller able to meet the needs of the brokers' clients, however large they might be.

It was a fundamental rule of the old system that brokers could not deal with each other and jobbers could not deal direct with the general public. This separation was carried to its logical extreme in the ban on 'mixed marriages' between brokers' and jobbers' firms.

This 'single capacity' system of 'one firm, one function' may have suited conditions before the first world war, when Britain still appeared to be at the zenith of her world power. But, today, it has come to be seen as a slow and cumbersome way of doing business. But who knows whether the pendulum will one day swing back again and people will once more extol the virtues of specialisation?

The political pressures leading to deregulation of the Stock Exchange were considerable. The story began with a rather unsympathetic Labour government. In 1976, it made an order under the 1973 Restrictive Practices Act for the Stock Exchange to register its rule book with the Office of Fair Trading. The OFT later informed the Stock Exchange that it had found a number of restrictions as defined by the Act. These were: limits to the freedom of brokers to supply their services (i.e. minimum commissions were in force), limits to the operation of the market system (i.e. single capacity), and limits to the use of agents (i.e. controls on membership of the Exchange).

By 1981, the case was well under way and the prospect of a long and costly law suit faced both sides. The Stock Exchange had hoped that the election of the Conservative government in 1979 would provide some relief. But when Sir Nicholas Goodison, Chairman of the Stock Exchange, asked a Royal Commission to look into the matter of restrictive practices in the Exchange, his request was refused. He argued that a court was not the right forum for the matter, since it could only decide innocence or guilt. What was required was a body able to recommend improvements. The then Secretary of State for Trade and Industry, John Nott, felt that to make an exception for the Stock Exchange when the whole thrust of government policy was to sweep away restrictive practices would be quite inappropriate.

The End Of An Era

Many commentators date the City Revolution from July 1983, when John Nott's successor as Secretary of State for Trade and Industry, Cecil Parkinson, agreed with Sir Nicholas Goodison to exempt the Exchange from restrictive practices legislation on certain conditions, namely the abandonment of fixed minimum commissions and freedom of entry for outside firms. The route by which this agreement was reached was independent of the abolition of exchange controls, but it was probably inevitable once exchange control went because of the outflow of funds in search of cheaper dealing. Indeed, all sorts of informal discounting of commissions was already allegedly going on by brokers anxious to attract and retain the valued custom of the big institutions.

Behind the domino of fixed minimum commissions stood that of single capacity, and it went down very quickly. Basically, if there was to

The Stock Exchange building: scene of the Big Bang on October 27th, 1986.

be a free-for-all in the pricing of their services, members needed to be free to earn money however they could. But again, one thing leads to another. If brokers were to expand successfully and safely into market making, that is dealing on their own behalf, they needed more capital. That could only come from merging with institutions which had it; so, as of March 1986, away went the rule which limited to 29.9% the size of the stake outside firms were allowed to own in member firms.

There was no shortage of outsiders keen to own their own brokerage or jobber. To date some sixty deals, involving huge sums, have been announced. The attraction of such marriages, from the point of view of the outsiders, is that they are buying expertise in a specialised market which would otherwise take them years to build up. An alternative approach followed by some was to set up the necessary subsidiary and then headhunt the talent needed to run it. The most skilled practitioners have been able to command colossal salaries and, not infrequently, 'golden hellos' the size of footballers' transfer fees as inducements to quit their current employer. More than one outside firm has found itself in the embarrassing position of having bought an existing member firm only to discover that most of the talent they thought they were getting had been poached by rivals. This problem has led to the quaint device of slipping 'Golden Handcuffs' onto key staff to retain their loyal service.

6
Foreign Competition

The intervention of foreign banks in the City is nothing new. But the trickle which began early this century has been gathering pace, with the numbers doubling in the last ten years to over 490. They employ a lot of people too, some 40,000, but they haven't impinged on the world of the man-in-the-street because they don't go in for High Street or retail banking. The earliest arrivals came simply to look after the banking needs of their own national companies trading with or through the UK. That didn't keep them busy for long; they began to look around for something else to do and have been doing it ever since.

From the 1960s they have been heavily involved in the eurocurrency markets and in such business as leasing and factoring. But they are also becoming a force to be reckoned with in Britain's domestic wholesale banking market; indeed, their share of sterling loans to British residents stood at over 21% in mid-1985. Their share of non-sterling loans was, predictably, a good deal higher at 75%. Besides these banks, the City plays host to a growing band of foreign securities firms now numbering about 120.

These overseas banks haven't simply brought over their local expertise. They have brought methods of doing business which are 'foreign' to the gentlemanly traditions of the City. As a result, the competitive climate has been hotting up not just through force of numbers but in terms of the savage cut-and-thrust tactics employed by the participants. One has only to look in the newspapers to see how the current merger mania has spawned a stream of aggressive advertisements; writs are flying faster than ever before.

The main source of these new tactics is undoubtedly the US. America's own financial revolution occurred in 1975, and it is they who have been making most of the competitive waves over the last decade. As we have seen, the institutions dealing in the main US financial markets are usually much bigger and better capitalised than their British rivals, and often more internationally minded — this despite the fact that the British international banking network is far larger and more comprehensive than the Americans'.

7
Domestic Competition — The Building Societies

Domestically, the competitive temperature has been turned up by the building societies. These venerable, non-profit institutions emerged in their thousands from the self-help mutual society movements of Victorian England. After the second world war, they took on a new lease of life as the main beneficiaries of postwar affluence. Now that millions of working people were well enough off to think of owning their own homes, and to save accordingly, the societies' coffers began to swell. Yet as recently as 1969 their deposits were smaller than the high street banks' — just. But since then, their share of total household deposits has almost doubled to reach 50%, putting them ahead of the high street banks by a substantial margin.

In addition, the subsidy to home ownership through mortgage interest tax relief has guaranteed the building societies ever-growing outlets for profitable lending. Through hundreds of amalgamations, the total number of societies now stands at something under 200. But, between them, they have 28 million depositors and 6 million borrowers, and the largest five societies account for more than half of all home loans.

However competitive the building societies have become today, they too have been tied in restrictive knots, partly of their own making and partly imposed upon them by statutes dating from the infancy of the movement. The societies' peculiar constitutions and quasi-charitable functions threw up some interesting prudential and administrative problems. These led to special regulation by government and justified — or so it was deemed — the formation of a strong Building Societies Association to oversee what had become a very powerful cartel in the home loan market.

A 'prudential ratio' sets out the proportion of a deposit taker's deposits that must be kept in certain approved assets, such as government bonds. Hitherto, it has been thought prudent to require the societies to hold much larger ratios than the banks, so that they will always have enough liquid assets to repay depositors on demand. This has now been changed.

The practice of setting agreed rates of interest has also been abandoned, as a result of increasing confidence and professionalism in the movement generally, combined with some pressure from more aggressive bankers invading their market. This has not quite led to a price war, but it has probably cut home loan rates a little and certainly benefited (rather belatedly) those home owners who have endowment linked mortgages and were being charged an extra ½% for the privilege.

Innovation has continued, and building societies are to be found leading some of the most significant developments in retail financial services in the 1980s, for example banking from home via the TV and telephone.

Financial Services Supermarkets

The general thrust of the societies' recent development has been towards providing a complete package of services at the retail level. In other words, they want a slice of the business which for years has been the exclusive preserve of the clearing banks. The provision of complete financial services packages is one of the recurring themes of the City revolution. It is what everyone is trying to do at whatever level they are trading. The old system of separate specialist services provided by separate organisations — money transfer by banks, share deals by stock brokers, insurance by Lloyd's and the insurance companies, and so on — is out. One-stop shopping is in with a vengeance.

For building societies to complete their transformation into financial services supermarkets, some big changes have to be made in how they are regulated. As we have seen, the process has already begun; the legislation needed to complete it went before Parliament in mid 1986 in the form of the Building Societies Bill. Above all the societies need to be able to make unsecured loans, just as the banks do. Then they will be able to move in on the commercial banks' pitch in a big way.

Regulation has not been the only rein on the growth of the societies. They have had to contend with the grip of the clearing banks upon the national money transfer system via the London Bankers' Clearing House. Membership of this exclusive institution was, until recently, confined to the Bank of England and the Big Four. Gradually it has enlarged to include Coutts, the Trustee Savings Bank, National Girobank and the Coop Bank. Several rank outsiders have also been hammering on the door to gain admission and reorganisation is under way to permit that.

But what will they gain admission *to*? Not, as it once was, a room in which soberly suited gentlemen solemnly swapped bundles of cheques.

For, increasingly, the transfer of money is taking place electronically. Of course, as long as cheques go on being used, cheque swapping will be needed, as will a convenient place in which to do it. But most money transfer in Britain will soon be electronic. Hence the interest being shown by building societies in EFTPOS (Electronic Funds Transfer At Point Of Sale — a system for debiting customers' bank accounts at the moment that they buy goods or services).

The commercial world into which these new financial supermarkets will emerge is, as we have said, changing rapidly. The small specialist is being displaced by the large conglomerate offering complete packages. This is happening in part because it's what the customer wants. But the customer also wants high quality service, which means reliable up-to-the-minute information and advice and speedy execution of his wishes — all, of course, at the lowest possible price. Competition has already forced the clearing banks to cut their account charges for private customers. This in turn has put pressure on them to make better use of their expensive branch networks by selling specialist services supplied by separate subsidiaries, for example insurance.

8
The New Technology

Rothschild's Bank grew to its nineteenth century pre-eminence largely because its information network was better than that of its competitors. Nathan Rothschild learned the result of the Battle of Waterloo a full day earlier than his rivals and was able to position himself in the market accordingly. Information, now as then, is money.

The difference between then and now, however, is the enormous volume of information available today to anyone who can afford to plug into the various financial news services. In the past, banks which knew all there was to know about their customers were in a strong position to advise them and to provide them with the services they required. Now such information is available on screen about all big companies. Anyone can call up that information and use it to put together a package of proposals tailored to a particular company's needs. It is then a matter of lifting the phone and making a sale. The traditional stable relationship between a banker and his client can be lost through competition in minutes.

Technology has made its impact on every facet of the financial world, and it is worth looking at some of the changes being wrought in the various institutions. Indeed, technological change is arguably the foremost influence behind the Big Bang.

The Stock Exchange

The London Stock Exchange is a market place where buyers and sellers meet to transact business in shares and bonds. At its simplest, it is a market with a physical location in the City, where buyers and sellers really do meet face-to-face to haggle and bid (in a gentlemanly sort of way) and can get the 'feel' of the market.

It is a special market in one significant respect — it has been closed to all but registered members of the Stock Exchange. It is run *by* them and *for* them and, not surprisingly, it had in its rule book certain rules expressly designed to keep the price of the services that members offer (i.e. buying or selling shares) higher than might be the case if anyone were allowed to set up as a broker. This is what fixed minimum commissions were about: *all* brokers charged the same fixed commission to all their customers.

Big institutional users of the brokers' services became increasingly discontented with fixed commissions. After all, much of the business they did was high volume, low risk; they felt that they should get a discount for bulk purchase. In particular, the accepting houses (a prominent group of merchant banks) felt that, as no redress for their grievance was forthcoming from the Stock Exchange itself — which resolutely defended fixed commissions — they would seek a technological answer to their problems.

The result was ARIEL — Automated Real Time Investment Exchange Limited — which provided communication between subscribers at two levels. Information about bids and offers could be input into the system and would appear on all VDUs. Any subscriber wishing to buy could contact the seller directly through the system. The institutions could thus buy and sell from each other directly, avoiding *any* payment of commissions to brokers or margins to jobbers.

This was a disturbing development for the Stock Exchange and, indeed, for the government. Both feared that the market for stocks and shares would fragment. It could become difficult and complicated to control and use. The Stock Exchange therefore tried to buy out ARIEL and to cut its members' commissions to institutional buyers to make their services more competitive. The government itself boycotted ARIEL and continued to trade gilts through the Stock Exchange in the traditional way.

Eventually, ARIEL was amalgamated with other information systems and lost its dealing facility. But the Stock Exchange had to 'buy it out' by ceding to the accepting houses some say in the affairs of the market — hitherto the jealously preserved sanctum of brokers and jobbers only.

Foreign Exchange Markets

It was in providing a *dealing* facility that ARIEL truly threatened the Stock Exchange. Simple information systems, perhaps with the ability to change the information at the orginator's request, had been around for a long time (Reuters, Extel, Datastream for example). These services were and are used extensively in foreign exchange markets; the different currencies could conveniently be displayed on one screen, and dealers could flick from page to page searching for another financial institution that was offering a price that they found acceptable. Dealing itself could then be done perfectly easily by telephone, as all the participants were institutions of considerable financial standing with credit ratings that were beyond doubt.

Over-The-Counter Markets

Over-the-counter shares are shares in companies that are too small or too new to warrant a Stock Exchange listing. They are therefore brought to the market by dealers who will trade with anyone. There is no need to trade through the offices of a stockbroker: the shares can be bought 'over the counter'.

The development of the NASDAQ (National Association of Securities Dealers' Automated Quotation) system in the US to facilitate OTC deals has revolutionised the way the market operates there. The corresponding system in the UK (SEAQ — Stock Exchange Automated Quotation System) promises to do the same here.

These systems provide three levels of service. First, there is a display of representative prices of the shares that are being offered for sale. This information can be made available to the general public. The second level, available only to dealers in the market, can display a list of all market makers and their bid and offer prices, together with information about the volume of shares they are willing to trade. The third permits the market makers to feed in changes in the price and volume that they are willing to accept.

For the most part the bargains are struck by telephone, but NASDAQ has developed a fully automated system for dealing in small batches of shares where no telephone call is necessary; sales can be made directly through the computer terminal (the Computer Assisted Executive System). There is, of course, no theoretical reason why this system should not be extended to large purchases of shares by credit-worthy institutions.

It is clear that the new technology in almost all markets threatens traditional trading methods and relationships. There are some who maintain that a successful dealer will owe his success to the 'feel' of the market — a feel which can only be obtained by personal contact and the excitement of the physical market place. Even this is called into doubt. NASDAQ can now display the price of deals in each share within seconds of the deal having been completed. Dealers ought to be able to get even the 'feel' of the market from their VDUs — as foreign exchange dealers obviously must.

The High Street Banks

One of the most conspicuous ways in which the banks have already introduced their customers to the sharp end of technology, with enormous success, has been to install Automated Telling Machines (ATMs). From the banks' point of view, ATMs promise to reduce payrolls and the costs of any financial transaction. The traditional high street presence, even, may not be required in the future by many of the banks' retail customers, with serious implications for these multi-branch giants. If all that is needed is a hole in a wall for an ATM, any retail chain might want to provide the service.

Home banking also becomes a force for change as does EFTPOS. In theory, it should be possible to develop a completely cash-free, and perhaps even cheque-free, society where all credits and debits can be handled electronically.

Control room from which Lloyds Bank monitors over 1000 Cashpoint machines (ATMs) throughout the UK.

The commercial banks can now provide better services for their corporate clients as well. The reach of most firms is increasingly international. They want detailed market information on the countries into which they sell, including credit appraisal of their customers. They also want management of their foreign exchange liabilities, their cash position at home and overseas, their debt capital structure and so on. The technology now exists to provide all this. The banks may well be forced to compete qualitatively for their clients' accounts as well as quantitatively in terms of cheap services and high interest on positive balances.

In responding to the challenge of technology, the banks face formidable problems. First, it is imperative that all banks (perhaps in all countries) should use standardised equipment and procedures so that money transfer can be fully automated. But such cooperation is more problematical than might appear: they are after all competitors. If one bank has a strong branch network, then assisting another, which hasn't, by giving it the freedom to promote its business everywhere may appear unwise.

A second problem is security. Already the high cost of credit card borrowing (where at least a signature is required) in part reflects the burden of fraud losses. How much more would be lost if only a PIN (Personal Identification Number) was needed to authorise a purchase?

Eager though the banks may be for technological innovation, they have to carry their customers with them if their profits are to rise. Weaning their current account customers off cash and cheques for everyday purchases and on to electronic banking is a daunting task.

The potential benefits from overcoming these problems are, however, enormous in terms of cost savings and the opportunities opened up for drawing new customers into the banking net. A cheaper, better, newer service may well appeal to that large minority who still do without the services of a high street bank.

The Tide Of Technology Carries All Before It

The silicon chip has generated most of the changes which present such a challenge to the City in the 1980s. Even push-button telephones are old fashioned in today's City. By merely touching a VDU screen with a pen, dealers in London can call up dealers in New York instantly: they don't have to wait like the rest of us while some non-existent telephone dial clicks round registering the numbers. The days are past when hopeful share buyers waited while their brokers legged it from the phone to two or three jobbers' pitches on the floor of the Stock Exchange to find out prices: the answer is on the screen beside the broker's telephone.

Lloyds Bank's new centralised dealing room.

Technology provides easier and cheaper ways of carrying out routine operations in bulk and at speed. It also makes possible (usually quite cheaply) things that were once impossible at any price. It thus creates new services and forces up minimum standards in the provision of existing services. But the use of the expression 'cheap' needs a word of qualification. Typically, technology reduces the average cost of producing anything, provided that the equipment is kept fully occupied; but it vastly raises the start-up costs of the business.

The installation costs of the gadgets being brought into use in the City are monumental. This fact alone means that size of operation carries a premium in terms of efficiency and thus profitability. The cost does not just arise from the hardware — to set up a dealing room and its supporting offices you could easily get through £15 million. The whole building will probably need gutting to allow the modifications needed to house all that tackle. Tucking away the 150 miles or more of extra cable needed by so much gadgetry poses more problems than merely how to stop people tripping over it. So much heat is generated that you need a special air conditioning system as well. Not surprisingly, some companies have opted for purpose built offices as the most cost-effective approach.

9
Hence The Revolution

While the discussions between the DGFT and the Stock Exchange dragged on, in the early 1980s, the precariousness of the City's position became increasingly apparent. In 1982, for example, earnings from abroad of Stock Exchange brokerage fees actually declined in real terms, after allowing for inflation. But the Stock Exchange was trapped in its struggle with the Office of Fair Trading and unable to think about whatever changes in its practices might be needed. The deal with the government, by which the Stock Exchange was exempted from the restrictive practices legislation in return for the end of fixed minimum commissions and restricting membership, broke the log-jam.

Very soon, it became obvious to everyone in the City, that the floodgates had indeed been thrown open and that very far-reaching changes were rushing towards them. The Stock Exchange deliberately and wisely gave itself plenty of time in which to bring in the agreed reforms. Setting October 1986 as a target gave everyone a breathing space in which to plan for an orderly transition.

We have suggested that Mrs Thatcher's government more or less stumbled on the City Revolution. By abandoning exchange control, it sparked the revolutionary changes at the Stock Exchange, though they would have to have happened some time. But the government clearly did not conceive the thing from the start as a coherent plan of campaign. An inexorable chain of cause and effect took over as the forces of competition, accelerated by technological change, dictated the essential nature and direction of the changes to be made.

All this is not to say, however, that the government has been a helpless bystander since 1983. Economically, politically, and administratively, the City revolution appears to offer enormous benefits to government — perhaps especially to a Conservative one with radical pretensions. Understandably, therefore, Mrs Thatcher's government has been closely involved and not simply left things to the Bank of England.

On the economic front, with hindsight, there would appear to have been no alternative to some kind of City revolution. A strong City is essential. If — appalling thought — it was allowed to follow manufacturing into depression and decline through uncompetitiveness, the consequences for jobs and for the balance of payments would be serious indeed. Besides, a competitive financial sector is an essential foundation for regenerating the manufacturing sector; few would deny that such a regeneration has become one of our most urgent needs.

The political advantage of boosting competition in the financial sector comes in two forms: the attainment of a short term electoral objective and of a long term ideological dream. The sale of British Telecom was a success: it did for shareholding what council house sales did for property ownership. To be able to put your political creed into practice, and find it has electoral appeal too, must be every government's dream. Mrs Thatcher believes firmly in the efficacy of the free market to allocate resources so as to maximise the total welfare of citizens. She also needs to attract some electoral assets to set off the growing electoral liability of the dole queue, a queue which suggests that maybe not all markets allocate effectively when left to themselves. The more people who buy shares as a result of her privatisation policy, the fewer people there are left who can afford to vote for Labour to take them all back into public ownership again.

Administratively, the City Revolution poses two distinct challenges to the government, and in particular to its agent the Bank of England. Government expenditure has to be funded, and private enterprise has to be regulated. The upheavals at the Stock Exchange have given the Bank of England the chance to set up the kind of securities market it wants, one which will maximise its ability to sell government debt (i.e. bonds) under all circumstances at the best rates available.

While planning the reorganisation of the gilts market, the Bank has also been trying to build a regulatory framework for the entire City which will promote competitiveness, cause as little distortion as possible, and provide comprehensive investor protection — a combination of objectives made much more elusive by the present changes. The most widely discussed supervisory problems arise from conflicts of interest which may now occur much more easily. The new octopus-like financial conglomerates must keep their different 'arms' separated so that secret information about a client (which is known to, say, the people organising its defence against a takeover) cannot be used by the people giving advice to the portfolio managers of institutions such as insurance companies. These artificial separations are popularly known as 'Chinese walls'. It remains to be seen how well the system will work when the competitive heat is really turned up.

Conclusion

Much attention has been focussed on the Stock Exchange's Big Bang by the press and the media generally. They see something newsworthy, tangible, and relatively easy to explain, at least in broad outline, to a non-specialist audience. It would, however, be a mistake to give undue importance to the event itself. Nor should we emphasise the significance of the particular date on which the Big Bang officially occurs.

In many ways the Big Bang should be seen as the product of a revolution already well under way, rather than as a cause of that revolution. We have already seen that technology, new dealing practices in international capital markets, and government activity, made it extremely likely that the world financial system was due for a change. Indeed, most institutions were aware of the pressures for change and were responding accordingly, positioning themselves to seize the opportunities presented. Where regulation stood in their way they sought ways of avoiding such regulation, or of changing the structure of the market in which they were operating. They showed themselves to be reactive, innovative and dynamic, and well capable of instituting and managing change for their own benefit.

Government regulatory intervention into the marketplace is often not the cause of change: it is the consequence of it. Frequently, government trails behind changes that have happened and legislates retrospectively to tidy up a *fait accompli*.

The Big Bang is no exception. Well before the OFT began examining the official rule book of the Stock Exchange, the financial community was showing itself to be restless. When the 2% stamp duty on stock market transactions became irksome, the market devised the ADR to beat the system. The government consequently halved the stamp duty. When the accepting houses became fed up with paying large commissions to stockbrokers, they devised automated dealing via ARIEL.

The agreement finally reached between the Stock Exchange and the government pleased most of the City because it was obvious to them that major changes had to come. The final compromise was better than a prolonged legal battle. The government may claim that, without the threat of legal action, the City would never have carried out these essential reforms. But, though the government hurried matters along, the seeds of change and of the direction of change were sown long before.

In Part 2 we will consider the direction of change as it affects particular British institutions. We will begin with the investment banks, more commonly referred to in the UK as merchant banks. We begin here not because of their physical size in the UK financial system, but because of their importance in the revolutionary process. They, more than any other financial institution, have precipitated the changes through their innovative marketing strategies. It is worth looking in some detail at them since the early 1970s to see how this happened. We will discover that the City revolution is not so much an explosion, nor even a series of detonations, but rather an accelerating change in the climate that hastens both the evolution and the extinction of the dinosaurs of the financial system.

Part Two
The Institutions After the Big Bang

10
Investment Banks

The first dim rumblings of the financial revolution were heard more than a decade ago in the City offices of the investment banks. Traditionally, their business has been to earn fees on specialised services (for instance the management of a share issue or a take-over) and to make loans to companies.

British merchant banks have built up a sound reputation for good advice and expertise, and for responding effectively to their customers' capital needs. Typically, if a company wanted to raise money on the capital market, it would go to a merchant bank; the bank would then design a suitable issue of bonds or shares, making sure that what was proposed complied with City standards and regulations.

The bank would also arrange for the issue to be underwritten: when the bonds or shares are brought to the market, either the bank or its associates would guarantee (for a fee) to purchase any that were not immediately taken up. This is a valuable service for two reasons. It ensures that the client company will receive the full amount expected on the right date, and it avoids the risk of paper being left hanging around in the market waiting for buyers — a situation which hardly inspires confidence in the company.

Finally, the merchant bank would arrange for the distribution of the bonds or shares to those individuals and institutions that wished to buy them. The process took months and tended to be quite costly.

The Customer Knows Best

A number of factors made the merchant banks' corporate clients less and less satisfied with this service as time went on. First, world markets were becoming more volatile. As we have seen, the pursuit of a monetary solution to the problems of inflation led to interest rates fluctuating widely over time and between countries. Changes in exchange rate often meant that dealing in one currency was more profitable than dealing in another. Large firms began to realise that 'windows of opportunity' existed in world markets in the form of low interest rates and appreciating currencies, but only for short periods of time, and they own regulations to see if they could capture the success of the eurobond market for their own domestic use. They came up with Rule 415.

Rule 415 permits large companies to pre-register new issues with the Securities Exchange Commission (SEC), and to put them on the shelf for up to two years. This gives them the freedom to bring the issue to market when they feel the time is right and to invite bids from the banks. This has given the big companies far greater control of the timing of their note issues and thus the ability to exploit 'windows of opportunity'.

As far as the investment banks were concerned, Rule 415 placed an emphasis on size. The banks that could either buy outright (or become at least the lead manager of a bought deal) could then recoup the loss of fees that would have been earned under the old system by selling the issue profitably in the secondary market. What they needed was, first, enormous capital with which to purchase a bought deal; and, second, a very good distribution system through which to pass the issue on. The essence of this business was speed; to keep the issue for a long time tied up capital and threatened (in falling markets) a capital loss. Banks having good contacts with wholesale buyers of securities (the insurance companies and pension funds, for instance) did well, as did those who could pass on the securities through their own retail outlets to shareholders.

. . . And Britain As Well

In the UK, bought deals are not unknown, though as yet the corporate bond market is small. Companies have found the traditional form of bank lending (overdraft) or the eurobond market adequate for their needs. They have therefore placed much more emphasis on these forms of finance than have their American counterparts.

One thing is clear, however. If the bought deal is to become a feature in the UK domestic market, the investment banks will need to grow bigger to compete with the large American financial institutions. At the moment they are comparatively tiny.

The Government Gives A Push

If customer dissatisfaction with the old-style services provided by the merchant banks, together with the manifest success of the eurobond market encouraged them to revolutionise their business, governments too provided a stimulus.

The end of fixed commissions and the opening up of the Stock Exchange to outside competition has meant that now both commercial and merchant banks can engage in the distribution of securities which used to be the sole prerogative of the stockbrokers.

Price competition will surely increase, and brokers will find that the once lucrative process of charging fees for their services will become less and less rewarding. They will have to find other ways of making money and the end of single capacity gives them just the chance they need. If they become market makers, (deal on their own account rather than as agents for others) they stand a chance of making sufficient profit to replace their declining commission income. However, before they can become market makers, they need capital; they have therefore sought out other institutions who have capital but lack their expertise on the stock market and who wish to take their chance in the securities markets.

The investment banks have so wished. As a result, the deregulation of the Stock Exchange has precipitated not just a landslide of mergers between stockbroking firms and other financial institutions but also a revolution in outlook for the investment banks. They are used to dealing in the eurobond market and in the American securities market and are now positioning themselves to use the skills thus developed in the UK domestic market.

The commercial banks have considerable financial muscle. They tend to be much bigger in terms of both capital and cash than the investment banks, and are also interested in becoming market makers now that deregulation has opened the way. But, as investment banking business moves away from the fee-earning services and towards the bought deal, even the combined resources of a stockbrokerage and a UK merchant bank will still only produce a fairly small fish in the international securities pond. The implication is clear. Either the investment banks must get bigger still or they will be pushed aside by the bigger commercial banks, and by US and Japanese securities houses, in the battle for business in the securities markets.

Small Is Beautiful

There is, of course, an alternative. Traditionally, merchant banks have built their success on a detailed knowledge of one particular aspect of the financial process or of a particular group of customers. Some are regarded as experts in defending against take-overs, some in arranging them; some limit the number of their clients so that they can give a very personal service; and so on.

But traditional loyalties are being eroded. In the past, a company used only a few merchant banks, perhaps only one. But with the globalisation of the market place, and the increasing sophistication of corporate treasury departments, shopping around for the best service is becoming commonplace. Companies no longer assume that the bank they normally deal with will necessarily provide the best service. They will approach specialists whose reputations are high in particular areas to provide them with just the service they need. Investment banks will have to develop more aggressive marketing strategies if they are to continue to earn high fees. They will have to persuade beady-eyed corporate treasurers that their products really are unique and better than any available world-wide. Already the cold call has replaced the old school tie as the basis for drumming up new business, and corporate treasurers are besieged by more enthusiastic salesmen from the investment banks than they can handle.

Into The Future

Two important trends are now bringing about a complete change in the orientation of London merchant banks. First, as the world market shrinks and deregulation allows banks of all kinds from every country to compete for business everywhere, their traditional earnings from fee-

BANKS	BROKERS	JOBBERS
Barclays	De Zoete & Bevan	Wedd Durlacher
Midland (Samuel Montagu)	W. Greenwell	
National Westminster	Fielding Newson-Smith	Bisgood Bishop & Co.
Kleinwort Benson	Grieveson Grant	Charlesworth & Co.
S.G. Warburg	Rowe & Pitman Mullens	Akroyd & Smithers
Hill Samuel	Wood Mackenzie	
N. M. Rothschild	Scott Goff Layton & Co.	Smith Bros.
Orion	Kitcat & Aitken	
Morgan Grenfell	Pember & Boyle	Pinchin Denny
Security Pacific	Hoare Govett	C. T. Pulley
Merrill Lynch		A. B. Giles & Cresswell

Some City mergers since 1983.

yielding services are likely to be threatened. The profitable end of the market is now in dealing. To do this, the banks need to be in a position to buy and hold securities until the price is right and a sale can be arranged. Capital is the key and the merchant banks therefore need to tie in with financial institutions that have it. The merger mania of the past few years has been clear evidence of this need.

If the resulting financial conglomerates are to compete with American giants like Merrill Lynch and Saloman Bros, they are going to have to provide a complete range of products more or less 'off the shelf'. Large American banks now anticipate their customers' needs by buying in stocks of the financial assets they feel might be required. To compete with this, the new British conglomerates will need both financial muscle and the skill and verve of American bankers — who, it must be admitted, have been playing the game for much longer.

The second factor influencing the development of UK investment banks is that banks world-wide will be judged on the quality of the services they provide and the suitability of the products they offer. If the financial conglomerates must be supermarkets in order to survive in securities markets, they must also be boutiques if they want to keep the fee-earning business of advising their clients. If they do not, they will lose out to smaller, specialist firms that can provide, say, the best contested take-over advice in the world.

As customers shop around for the best they can find, banks must compete by offering newer, cheaper products individually tailored to their customers' needs. A brief look at some of the products that have been developed since the 1970s in the bond market will provide an illustration.

Floating Rate Notes (FRNs)

These were developed in response to the market's lack of enthusiasm for traditional fixed rate securities when interest rates began to fluctuate widely in the 1970s. Interest rates are adjusted periodically throughout the life of a bond, giving the issuer and the purchaser confidence that the effective rate of interest will not be seriously out of line with market rates for long.

Note Issuance Facility (NIFs)

A lead bank arranges that its client's short term paper is underwritten as and when required. This gives the client certainty about the availability of money and allows him to borrow at short term rates of interest for what is effectively a medium term loan (because it can be rolled over).

Revolving Underwriting Facility (RUF)
This is the same as a NIF, except that if all the short term paper is not taken up by the market the bank guarantees to extend a conventional loan to make up the difference. Here again, the client has certainty of funds being available and the ability to borrow at (low) short term rates of interest.

Swaps
These take account of the fact that different borrowers have different credit ratings in different markets. An American company may be big enough to borrow at the lowest rates of interest from its bank at home but be unknown in the eurobond market. However, IBM can borrow cheaply in eurobond markets as it is well known and regarded as almost risk free. If IBM wants dollars in the US to pay its wage bill, and the American firm wants Deutschmarks to acquire a new European retail outlet, each can borrow where it can raise funds most cheaply and simply swap interest payments, splitting the saving between them.

High Yield Bonds ('Junk' Bonds)
These allow companies with poor credit ratings to raise money without borrowing more from their banks. They are, of course, more risky, but experience has shown that the high yields offset the occasional failure to pay interest or capital. Junk bonds are an American animal and have been used with conspicuous success by corporate raiders in contested take-overs. The game is to obtain a facility to raise capital by the sale of junk bonds, using as security the assets of the company that is about to be taken over. If the takeover bid is successful, then the junk bonds are sold and the victim company can be acquired.

Convertible Bonds
These offer the possibility of converting the bonds to equity capital (shares) when the bond matures.

Mortgage Bonds
Mortgages represent obligations to pay a specified rate of interest on a capital sum. In this way they are like bonds, and indeed mortgages can be aggregated into bond form and the rights they carry to payment of interest can be bought and sold like any other security.

11
The Commercial Banks

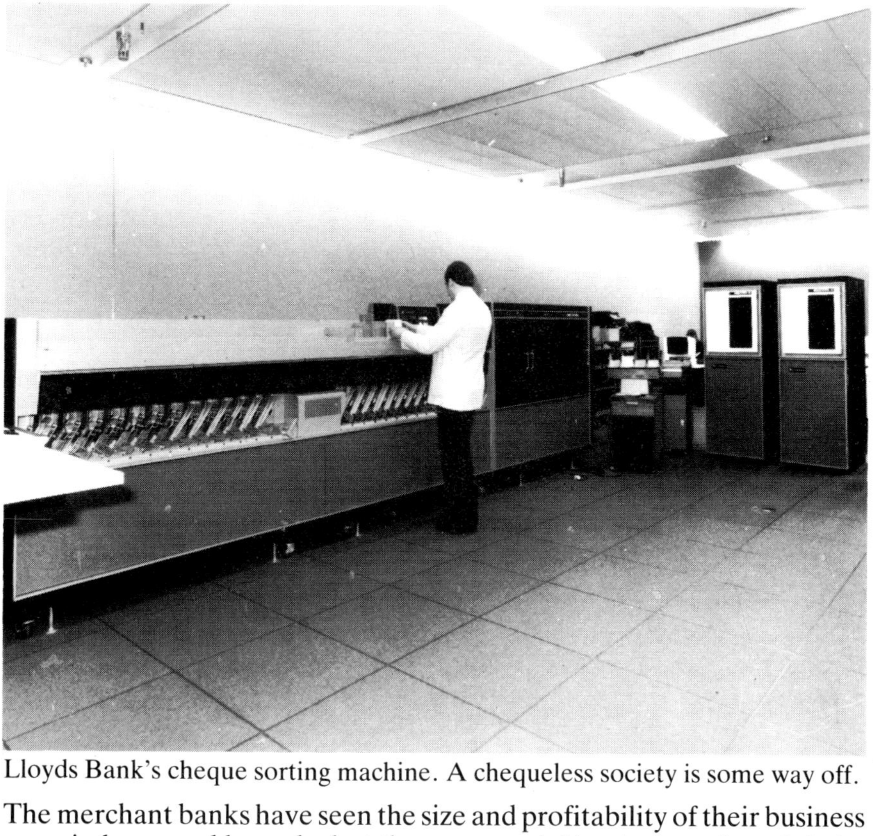

Lloyds Bank's cheque sorting machine. A chequeless society is some way off.

The merchant banks have seen the size and profitability of their business grow in leaps and bounds, but the commercial banks have found theirs to be under attack not only from almost every financial institution but from a few commercial and industrial corporations as well.

Governments have always recognised the special place that commercial banks have in the running of the economy. At a basic level, they facilitate trade by providing a safe, cheap chequing system which allows transactions to occur without costly and time-consuming cash handling.

The core business of commercial banks is relatively simple. They collect up money from those that have it (preferably at zero or low rates of interest) and lend it on to those that want it at a higher rate of interest. In fact, there is not a one-to-one relationship between original deposits and the quantity of loans that can be created. Banks can use their clients' funds to *create* money by extending loans to firms and individuals, which encourages both investment and consumption and so, ultimately, employment.

Let us consider what happens if two individuals, A and B, do a deal privately. If A lends £100 to B, A has lost the use of the money and B has gained it. There is still only £100 around. However, if A deposits his money in the bank, and the bank lends it to B, the effect is quite different. A can still write a cheque for £100 in favour of, say, C and the bank will move the money by means of computer entries to C's account. Meanwhile, B is also free to write a cheque for £100, as agreed with the bank, in favour of, say, D, and that money will be placed in D's account. So now we have C and D with £100 each, where before there was only £100 in all. It makes no difference whether there is one bank in the system or ten, so long as the money remains in the system, i.e. there is no hoarding.

This is, of course, a lucrative business and the banks' ability to conduct it depends on two things. First, they have to be sufficiently liquid to ensure that they can meet everyone's demand for cash; they have to get their liquidity ratio right. Second, there must be sufficient customers wanting to borrow the money.

The Problem of Liquidity

If the banks create too much credit, this may be inflationary. Furthermore, if they lend unwisely and their debts become uncollectable, then, in the end, they will run out of cash with which to honour the cheques drawn on the accounts held with them. This is the very worst situation that can occur. It can cause a 'run on the bank' where depositors, anxious lest their money should be locked into the bank on the day it finally fails, rush to draw funds out. In doing so, they make the bank's failure even more certain. If banks do fail, money is lost, as is faith in the whole system, with consequent ill effects on household spending and industrial investment and, in the end, on employment.

For these reasons, governments have been at pains to regulate banks to make sure they have a big enough capital base, and lend with sufficient prudence to avoid disaster. Their performance is regularly monitored by the Bank of England.

The most sensational series of failures in the American banking system happened after the Wall Street Crash of 1929. Banks had been lending to speculators on the security of the shares they were buying. When the stock market began to fall, the banks found that substantial borrowings were backed by bits of paper that were fast becoming worthless and they therefore called in their loans. The speculators found that, since they were now making capital losses, they were unable to repay the banks. The banks themselves failed, and what was in the first instance a 'little local difficulty' on Wall Street became an economic disaster of huge proportions as savings were lost and consumption collapsed.

The consequences of the 1929 crash still affect US commercial banks today. In the aftermath, the American authorities passed the Glass Steagall Act (1933) which forbade the commercial banks from dealing in bonds in an attempt to keep them insulated from the vagaries of the market.

However, American commercial banks are now increasingly discontented with the restrictions of the Glass Steagall Act. They have watched investment banks earning profits in the bond market beyond the dreams of avarice and also seen their best customers wooed away by the investment banks who are able to offer them cheaper and more flexible money.

Eager to dip their spoons in the cream too, the American commercial banks are both indirectly and directly challenging the Glass Steagall Act. The indirect approach is to arrange 'private placements' whereby, rather than purchasing an issue outright as in a bought deal — thus acting as principals — they act as agents, using their knowledge of their customers to place an issue with people who wish to buy. It is in practice an introduction service: the bank acts as matchmaker between the borrower and the lender, and charges a fee for its services.

The direct approach is simply to *do* the business and challenge any attempt to enforce Glass Steagall in the courts.

In Britain, similar activity can be seen. When government regulations on the volume or direction of bank lending were particularly obnoxious, the banks went on finding loans for their customers by introducing prospective borrowers to lenders and charging an agent's fee. Open defiance of the Bank of England is, however, *not* an option.

If making loans has been the traditional preserve of the commercial banks, and dealing in securities that of the investment banks, then the former has made a fairly determined effort to erode the position of the latter. Bank loans can now look so much like the sale of securities that you can hardly tell them apart.

Suppose, for example, Bank A is 'fully lent'. Because of government restrictions and prudential considerations, it can therefore take on no more lending. Suppose, as well, a potentially valuable customer approaches the bank with a request to borrow. The bank is, of course, loath to say no. Suppose, finally, there is another Bank B, with lending capacity to spare, and which is only too anxious to earn interest on this capacity. Bank A could, of course, push its customer on to B, but this would not be very wise in the long term. An alternative is to make space for the new customer's loan by calling in other loans, but this is likely to cause bad blood between the bank and its existing customers. The best solution, therefore, is to bundle up sufficient loans to make space and sell them off to Bank B. What is being transacted is a document which gives B the right to the interest and capital payments of A's customers, but the important thing to note is that such documents enable Bank A to offer a loan to its customer — indeed, effectively they *are* bank loans.

This process is called 'securitisation', and the commercial banks are increasingly keen to extend their activities into dealing in securities, partly because it is lucrative, and partly because they want to give their clients the fullest possible banking service.

A Shortage of Customers

We noted earlier in this section that profitable banking depends upon maintaining adequate liquidity and having enough customers. The experience of the Great Crash showed how closely these two requirements are linked. In the present age, there has been a similar significant event which has affected both the number of customers coming forward who wish to borrow, and the number who wish to deposit — the international debt crisis. This crisis has menaced the very jugular of the banks' existence and justifiably evoked fearful memories of the Great Crash.

The International Debt Crisis

The oil shock of 1973 completely overturned world-wide money flows, by giving the oil states enormous surpluses of cash and landing the rest of the world with corresponding shortages of it. At first things went well for the commercial banks. The oil states were not slow to realise that to sit on such a cash mountain could threaten to kill the golden goose. The economies of their Western customers could not sustain such a cash drain without it cutting their level of consumption. Less consumption meant less output, and less output meant less demand for oil.

The oil sheiks also realised that aside from the urgent need to recycle oil revenues back to the West, the process could also be pleasantly rewarding.

The large commercial banks were the main beneficiaries of this realisation. They were ideally placed to manage the reverse flow of petrocurrency and to place it where it was most needed. The mechanism used was the syndicated loan; a group of banks would borrow a huge sum of money from the oil states and lend it on to those who needed it.

In fact, it was the developing countries that were most in need. Rich countries had responded to the balance of payments difficulties, caused by rocketing oil prices, by deflating their economies. They engineered falls in national income in order to reduce their citizens' ability to buy imports. The developing countries in turn faced declining orders from rich countries for primary products, as well as vastly higher oil bills.

The banks therefore lent to the developing countries with an enthusiasm which seems, with the benefit of hindsight, to have been reckless to say the least. Experience had suggested that sovereign nations didn't go bust and so the banks were prepared to lend to them without putting them through the credit appraisals that would be normal practice in the domestic market. They also lent to big companies and institutions in these countries without, in all cases, making adequate appraisal of their creditworthiness.

While the business lasted, it was extremely profitable. But the business did not last — or, if it did, not in a way that the banks desired. Oil prices doubled yet again in 1979 and rates of interest rose sharply. In the early 1980s it soon became clear that some countries were having difficulty not just in repaying the borrowed capital, but even in servicing the debt. Some even had to borrow more money to pay interest on the existing debt. World recession had taken its toll on the borrower countries' ability to sell their exports, and hence on their ability to raise the dollars they needed to honour their obligations to the banks.

Quickly, the syndicated loan business dried up as the banks began to realise the risk of further lending. But by then it was too late. Some banks had already lent the equivalent of their entire equity capital to one or two countries. The IMF and the US Federal Reserve Board now became involved and top secret negotiations with debtor governments began. The banks made the painful discovery that the only way they could have any hope of extricating themselves was to go in deeper still.

In short, in order to prevent countries from defaulting the banks lent even more, or they 'rescheduled' debts by extending the repayment time or reducing the effective rate of interest. They feared that a default in one country would lead to others following suit, with the possibility of creating an enormous quantity of unrecoverable debt with unspeakable consequences for their balance sheets and reputations.

Pastures New

With the collapse of lending to developing countries, banks clearly needed to find new customers and so they turned their attention back to the developed world.

There were, however, several factors that made this market a tough nut to crack. First, as we have seen, the banks' traditional corporate customers — those who might have once used their syndicated loan service — were now finding the securities markets were producing an enormous array of cheap and efficient finance.

In the US, the banks' best customers were large companies which enjoyed a high credit rating. These companies were using securities markets almost exclusively, rather than borrowing in the normal way. Banks were therefore being forced down market: they had to lend to companies with lower credit ratings. The development of junk bonds has threatened even this business. But quite apart from that, it was clear that the profits earned by the investment banks from selling their new products were almost twice as large as those of the commercial banks. All this was a persuasive argument for diversification into capital markets.

What happens in the US often presages what is to follow in the UK. But the British overdraft system has so far proven to be a flexible and convenient form of finance, so that sales of bonds as an alternative may well be slow to catch on. But catch on it will.

The Cultural Revolution

A second problem facing commercial banks wishing to diversify is their lack of experience in the securities field. The skill of a commercial bank is to assess *credit* risk (whether the customer will be able to repay), whereas the skill of an investment banker is to assess *market* risk (whether the price of the bond will rise or fall).

On the face of it, the commercial banks have a lot going for them in their pursuit of the lucrative securities market. Their financial clout enables them to take a position in a market and to weather the storm if prices move against them. They also have a well-developed system of retail distribution. Many small purchasers of shares use their bank's stockbroking facilities, and if we are moving towards a share-owning democracy it should be possible for the commercial banks to exploit this advantage by selling piecemeal the shares they have bought in bulk from the market. They also have good contacts among both the likely issuers of securities and the big institutions that might buy them. They can therefore act as middlemen in arranging swaps, as well as providing an in-house securities service for their customers.

However, since the commercial banks lack the expertise in securities that the investment banks have established over the past two decades, they have not been able to establish an evironment which is conducive to nurturing securities dealing. This they will now have to do, but it will not be easy.

Commercial bankers have the benefits of working for a big organisation. Their salaries are generous but not extravagant; their career offers a steady progression and considerable security; their virtues are care, accuracy, caution, acumen and patience. Merchant bankers are rather different. Their life is more pressured and perhaps more glamorous. They need the ability to act immediately, imaginatively and confidently. They tend to enjoy much higher salaries coupled with much lower job security. There is a culture gap between the two.

If the commercial banks are to launch a successful assault on the securities markets, they need to recruit and keep good investment bankers, and this will inevitably produce a different managerial ethos. They need to develop an environment within their organisation that will permit the investment bankers to flourish.

The timing of the official Big Bang posed another problem for the commercial banks in that it placed a specific time limit on the development of a securities dealing division. After 27th October, commercial banks could compete with each other in the domestic capital market quite freely, and if they wanted to become market leaders they had to get a foot in the door at the earliest opportunity. They have had not much more than three years (since the historic Goodison-Parkinson handshake) to grasp this opportunity.

The route they have mostly chosen has been to buy in expertise from outside by forming conglomerates composed of the banks themselves with their financial and distributional skills, together with stockbrokers, merchant banks and stockjobbers who provide the market expertise which the parent bank lacks. How far these enterprises will succeed remains to be seen. They will have to demonstrate to the users of the market that they can provide a service as good, both in terms of price and quality, as the large American investment banks and the Japanese securities companies.

The Customers Take The Initiative

One pretty safe prediction is that the securities markets are likely to develop in Britain much as they did in the US. Large British companies, with good credit ratings, are finding that the cost of their overdraft facility compares unfavourably with the cost of selling bonds on world markets. As the recession ends and companies become more profitable, they will build up cash surpluses which at the same time reduce their need for bank borrowing and, in turn, cause them to think about alternatives to depositing their balances with their bank.

Large firms now tend actively to manage their cash assets for themselves, and to diversify into financial markets. Cash is no longer seen as just a by-product of their business which can be left in the bank, but rather as a valuable resource out of which they can create profit. Department stores issue their own credit cards, and may move into automated telling; big oil companies buy and sell securities, and at least one is in the forefront of EFTPOS technology; and airlines speculate in foreign exchange. Some firms may well find that these ancillary financial services are more lucrative even than their core business. After all, it has happened before: that is how the original merchant bankers came to be bankers and not merchants. To retain such customers, the banks must compete not simply with each other but with their customers' own in-house finance divisions.

Even the banks' smaller customers are beginning to look more critically and selectively at the services they are being offered. Traditionally, the small saver has been conservative in the management of his funds and has used deposit accounts in building societies as a sink for his savings. Over the years, investment trusts, unit trusts, insurance companies and others have been able to offer better yields and the chance of capital growth. If the liberalisation of the Stock Exchange and the privatization of the nationalised industries lead to cheaper dealing facilities and wider share ownership, savers may choose to buy shares directly on the Stock Exchange rather than use deposit accounts. Banks have therefore had to compete for funds with such other institutions, hence the growth of interest-bearing current accounts and the plethora of services that the banks now provide. They have found that, if they wish to keep their customers, they need to diversify into non-bank business such as insurance and unit trust schemes.

Conclusion

Banks today face an uncertain future. On the one hand, the traditional lending business is drying up because customers are finding other

A City branch of a clearing bank: a financial services supermarket already?

sources of supply. Small customers use credit cards, or borrow directly from the store where they buy their goods. Large customers enter the capital markets and, if they need advice at all, tend to approach the investment banks.

On the other hand, the *source* of bank funds is drying up too, as small customers shop around among an almost bewildering array of institutions willing to manage their savings. Large customers invest their money directly in the securities markets.

Banks have therefore felt the need to diversify by buying their way into the capital markets and by providing a wider spread of services for their small customers. This is taking place at a time when new technology produces both the problems and the opportunities we have seen earlier.

The banks have great strengths both in their size and in access to their customers through the branch networks. They have also shown themselves to be resilient and prepared to adapt to changing market conditions. But at the end of the day their success depends on whether they can beat the investment bankers at their own game.

12
The Building Societies

Traditionally, the building societies have enjoyed enormous success not so much because of their skills as money lenders but because of the special nature of the market in which they operate.

The chief influence on this market has been government policy, encouraging ordinary savers to invest in houses rather than other assets. There is tax relief on mortgage interest payments and no capital gains tax is payable on the appreciation of owner-occupied houses used as a main residence. This goes a long way to explain the buoyant demand for housing in recent decades, which has resulted in such sensational increases in house prices. These increases in turn amplify the flow of funds into housing and away from other forms of investment.

Another factor which has provided building societies with good business has been the changing social behaviour of the British population. More young people now leave home and set up separate establishments than ever before; as society grows increasingly affluent, more of them will be able to buy their own property, or at least meet the interest payments that their mortgages require.

A third influence has been the regulatory framework within which the market for housing finance has had to operate. This has had the effect, until recently, of locking out all competition, leaving the building societies free to enjoy a comfortable monopoly. Before 1971, monetary controls prevented the savings and commercial banks from providing mortgage finance; the building societies reinforced their supremacy by developing their expertise and a very comprehensive distribution network.

Since then, things have changed, but probably not as much as they will in the future. The building societies' monopoly has gone. Gradually, throughout the 1970s, the monetary authorities came to realise that the traditional way of controlling the money supply (by directly controlling bank lending) was no longer possible. If the government wanted to encourage the expansion of industry rather than house purchase, it could insist that the commercial banks lend only to expanding industrial companies. But the likely effect is simply to drive money out of the (controlled) banking system and into another (uncontrolled) sort of financial institution — the process known as disintermediation. Thus, if people wanted to buy homes rather than have their money invested in companies, they simply placed their savings with the building societies and not with the banks.

The position now is that, rather than trying to control the volume and direction of the flow of funds through banks, the authorities merely bring about adjustments in the general level of interest rates to encourage or discourage borrowing throughout the whole range of financial institutions. This is seen as being fairer since it does not discriminate against the institutions that were formerly subject to control, and as more likely to promote competition between different institutions for the same business. It does not, of course, remove the bias against investment in industry caused by the tax relief: if anything, it accentuates it by increasing the number of institutions competing to push money into the housing market.

As far as the building societies are concerned, the changes that occurred in the 1970s meant that the banks began to move into the housing finance market, partly because it was lucrative, enabling them to make fuller use of their expensive branch networks, and partly because it was also likely to generate additional business for their other operations, for example their insurance business.

A fourth important impetus for change in the housing finance market has been the development of the securities markets. Traditionally, the building societies have collected up money from individuals through their chain of outlets. In order to persuade customers to part with their savings, the societies have had to offer a rate of interest high enough to compete with the rates paid on other deposit accounts. But the societies can now borrow money much more cheaply than this in the eurobond market.

This means that the very basis of the success of the societies', namely their ability to gather savings through their distribution network, suddenly becomes a rather less valuable asset than it was before. If money can be found more cheaply, without employing people to staff outlets, why bother?

Faced with what to do with their retail outlets, the building societies have found that technology provides both a spur and a solution. Banks now provide both housing finance and banking and ancillary facilities, and if the societies are to compete they in turn must expand their cash transfer services. Already the societies are offering their customers cheque books, personal loans (backed by a mortgage agreement), automatic telling machines and insurance services. From the customers' point of view, it is getting harder and harder to tell the difference between a bank and a building society.

Until now, the building societies had been limited by law as to the range of services they could provide. But the new Building Societies Act gives them greater freedom to compete both inside the housing finance market and outside it. The Act comes into force in 1987, and will then, for the first time, allow the societies to lend a proportion of their total assets without security. They will be able to compete with the banks at every level. It is anticipated that the societies will provide at least some, if not all, of the full range of services itemised by the Act: foreign exchange dealing, making or receiving payments as agents, conveyancing, insurance broking, estate agency services, arranging pension schemes, and so on.

Fragmentation of the Market for Housing Finance

At present, the building societies handle the entire process of arranging the transfer of funds from those who wish to lend to those who wish to buy houses. This work actually comprises three distinct functions. These are:

1. Originating the mortgage loan; this means assessing the borrower's credit worthiness, and introducing the borrower to the lender;
2. Servicing the loan; arranging for the interest to be paid regularly to the lender;
3. Holding the loan; someone actually has to provide the capital to be borrowed.

In the past, building societies have offered their customers a package of services which includes all three functions, and up to now their customers have been well content with the service they have received.

There is, however, nothing sacred about the building societies' way of doing business, and in other countries things are done quite differently. Things will soon be different in the UK, too.

Banking regulations in the United States prevent the development of a branch bank network. This means that, when funds are held in the money centres (New York and Chicago, for example) but the demand for home loans is elsewhere, perhaps in the developing sunshine states, the banks have no direct method of channelling funds to where they are needed. This led to the development of mortgage banks, institutions that simply originate and service mortgages without providing finance. Technology has given a spur to this process. A mortgage bank (or indeed any other institution that wishes to originate a mortgage, be it a house builder or an estate agent) simply sends his client's details electronically to a credit rating agency. If the customer appears able to service the debt, the mortgage is created there and then. Bundles of mortgages are then 'packaged' and sold off as securities to big institutions wanting to buy them wholesale. There is a good market for such paper. The risk associated with house lending is low and the rate of return is attractive.

The same kind of fragmentation — the separating of the functions of originating, servicing and holding mortgages — seems to be taking off in the UK. One important reason for this trend is the deregulation of financial institutions. As long as building societies had a monopoly in the market for housing finance, they could offer low rates of interest on deposits. But when the commercial banks entered the scene, interest rates were bid up. Big financial institutions have now become interested in the relatively high yields on these low risk investments, and they have muscled in for a share of the market. They are not, however, willing to take on the costs of a chain of retail outlets; they prefer to use others as agents to originate and service the mortgages. They just hold the loan.

Meanwhile, at the other end of the market, estate agents, too, have been finding that things have been changing, creating new opportunities. Mortgage shortages have come to an end, with the arrival of the banks in the market and the realisation that the market no longer depended on what savings were placed with the building societies. Money can be freely imported as and when it is needed from the wholesale money markets.

Estate agents were finding that more and more of their clients were young, without capital and in need of financial advice. If the estate agents were not well placed to give such advice, they were certainly able to put such knowledge to profitable use. In the nature of things, estate agents are often the first point of contact of a customer in need of a mortgage, so they are in with a head start. If they could originate one, they could charge a fee for doing so (and probably another for servicing the mortgage). They are likely to sell more houses as well. It clearly makes sense for the estate agents to be playing a more active role in the mortgage market.

The Future

The building societies face a much less comfortable but a much more exciting future. As their depositors become ever more aware of the many possible destinations for their savings — banks, unit trusts, investment trusts, insurance policies, stocks and bonds — and as these alternatives compete more and more for funds that would previously have been deposited unquestioningly with a building society, the societies are really going to have to fight to survive in the 1990s. If, as seems inevitable, government tax policy changes to remove the incentive to invest in housing rather than, say, in industry, then the traditional source of savings may all but dry up completely. However, raising money this way is labour intensive and therefore rather expensive, so the societies may well be happy to bid for most of their money in the wholesale markets. But they will need to develop the same kind of trading skills as the experienced investment bankers.

Branch networks are of course important for making contact with the customers in the first place, so the societies must keep them going. To do so profitably, they will need to develop other retail business to cover their overheads. So, in all likelihood, the societies will end up providing many if not all of the services currently available from the clearing banks. Indeed, they have a foot in the door already, with their formidable retail presence nationwide. Adding extra services to this network does not entail large new fixed costs (such as new premises), but it will need coordination. If, for instance, the societies are to develop money transfer services, they will have to arrange clearing between one another. Furthermore, as the societies have built up immense goodwill over the years, they are one of the first ports of call for new homebuyers. They will be well placed to do business with people just when they are most likely to need 'banking' services — unsecured loans for purchase of furniture, extra insurance, and so on.

The fragmentation of the market will itself be an impetus for change. Indeed, there are already signs of a new structure in the housing finance market. Estate agents have for some years played a key role in originating mortgages, often introducing their clients to the building societies. It is now quite feasible for these introductions to be done electronically from the estate agents' offices, as happens in the US, where they can originate mortgages on the spot for creditworthy customers. The Bank of Scotland found that, whilst it could service mortgages successfully and earn good commissions on the business for very little extra cost (for the most part, the work is repetitive and can be done by machine) it was unable to hold the loans. Its capital was too small to support the volume of mortgage business it wanted to do. It has therefore created a number of home loan syndicates which hold the loan whilst the bank itself simply services it.

As the American influence spreads across the Atlantic with the financial institutions attracted to the City by the opportunities created by the

Big Bang, it is odds-on that cash rich American companies will look hungrily at our market for housing finance. Interest rates on UK mortgages are acceptably high and the risk is (or has been in the past) minimal. They will be looking to buy mortgage securities enabling them to hold the loan without having the servicing function, which may be left to the building societies.

13
The Insurance Companies & Pension Funds

The insurance companies and pension funds have thrived on a tax system which has encouraged savers to use their services rather than to invest directly on the Stock Exchange. But government today believes that channelling funds through a handful of large institutions is likely to damage the success of the economy. These institutions are therefore going to find the climate for their operations becoming more difficult as government encourages individuals to make more adventurous provision for their retirement.

Instead of paying steadily into a life assurance scheme or a pension fund, people may decide to buy unit trusts, shares in investment trusts or government securities to name but three choices. Already, unit trusts are offering some products which yield high growth (aimed at those in work and who wish to build capital) and others which yield high income (designed for the retired). Information about the performance of such schemes is now becoming widespread; savers are finding that they compare well with the yields they can expect from life policies. As the tax incentives on insurance policies are reduced, more and more savers will invest elsewhere.

The Big Bang will give the companies much cheaper dealing facilities and help them choose between a wider variety of financial institutions with whom they can place their business. SEAQ will help them see whether their dealers obtain the best price possible; they will be able to shop around for the best advice and information service available. Already the tendency is for assurance companies to use more than one fund manager and to compare performances critically. In the advertising industry clients may change their agency quite often to get the benefit of new ideas or a particularly talented team. Fund managers, too, may find client companies switching between them as and when it suits.

14
Unit Trusts & Investment Trusts

An investment trust is a company which makes no product itself, but buys and sells shares in order to obtain a high return in terms of both income and capital growth. Individuals who want to invest in the stock market, but who don't have enough capital for a wide portfolio, find this form of investment attractive. By pooling their savings they can have them efficiently and professionally managed and obtain the common benefits of a wide portfolio. The share price of the trust, and the dividend it pays, are a measure of its success. Dealing in such shares tends to be slow, as the buyers are often interested in long term investment and do not sell very often.

Unit trusts are similar but whereas the investment trusts tend to manage a fixed quantity of capital, the unit trusts expand or contract depending on whether their unit holders invest more or withdraw from the market. An investment trust will sell (say) 1 million ordinary shares at £1 each and try to manage the £1m of capital so created, in order to generate a surplus; but the unit trusts may sell more units at any time, increasing the assets at their disposal. This depends on there being a net inflow of funds (i.e. more people buying units than selling). If the opposite happens the unit trust managers will find their capital base shrinking.

Both unit and investment trusts act as intermediaries between the saver and the user of the funds. As such they will receive the same benefits, and incur the same costs, as many other similar institutions as a result of the Big Bang. Dealing costs will be lower and competition for their business between the market makers higher. However, as investors become more discerning, and information about other, more direct, forms of investment becomes widespread, the trusts too will need to compete for funds that have, in the past, come their way almost by default of competition.

Already some trusts have begun to specialise in order to give investors some choice in the final destination of their savings. If for example the investor feels bullish about the Japanese economy, commodity or gilt edged prices, he can find a variety of unit trusts that specialise in these sectors. Ultimately, the investor may decide to choose not just the sector in which he wishes to invest, but the actual shares. If this happens, the trusts may find it much harder to maintain their growth record. They may start trying to market their products more aggressively, perhaps through the banks or building societies — perhaps even through teams of door-to-door salesmen.

Part Three
Markets After the Big Bang

15
The London Stock Exchange

Single Capacity

The single capacity dealing system has several advantages. Since it has worked well for 80-odd years, it is obviously capable of providing a consistent market and one in which both buyers and sellers have confidence. This is clearly important: any threat to the fluidity of the market — the risk that sellers won't find buyers or vice versa — could hinder the country's ability to raise finance for investment. Therefore, any change in the system is likely to be contentious to say the least.

Under the single capacity system, the market consists of brokers and jobbers who do completely different jobs. The brokers act on behalf of their clients and are simply buying agents. It is their task to go round the stock market finding the best price they can. To do this, they approach jobbers, who are the wholesalers of securities. Jobbers maintain a stock of securities (they usually specialise in a particular type), and when approached by the broker they quote two prices. The lower is the one at which they will buy and the higher at which they will sell.

Sometimes the jobbers will sell shares they do not have (going short), but this is not a cause of dismay. They can do this in the certainty that they will be able to buy later on to cover their position. Obviously, if they expect prices to fall, they may well go short in the hope of making a gain later on in the day. Conversely, going 'long' means buying shares without selling others to raise money to pay for them (often in anticipation of a price rise). Money brokers help them to maintain these positions. They will lend stock to jobbers who are short and, when they are long, lend money against the security of shares. The key point is that brokers act on behalf of their customers as retailers, whereas jobbers act for themselves as wholesalers.

Both groups have a vested interest in maintaining good relations with each other. Jobbers may even narrow their margins in order to keep the business of a persuasive broker. Brokers need the jobbers, to make sure there is always someone prepared to buy what they wish to sell and sell what they wish to buy. Matching supply and demand for shares is thus ensured.

The Stock Exchange floor: market makers operate from the hexagonal stands.

However, in recent years the continuity of the stock market has been threatened. Because of the distorting influence of Britain's tax structure, investment in shares has largely been channelled through the big institutions, and they tend to buy only 'safe' shares in well-established companies. Jobbers who have specialised in other sectors have therefore done badly and overall the number of jobbers has dwindled. 'Gaps' have developed in the market; that is, there are some sectors in which no jobber is prepared to quote a price.

It has also become clear that, as stockbrokers diversify away from their original function (as in the case where they manage or underwrite issues for their clients), they may well find a conflict of interest between their wish that the issue should go well, and their wish to offer sound advice to their customers about which shares to buy.

Similarly, a conflict of interest may arise from the fact that, in single capacity, most of the stockbroker's revenue comes from transacting business which follows from advice given to their clients; they may be tempted to persuade their clients to buy and sell more often than is strictly necessary or even desirable. This problem is not, of course, peculiar to stockbroking. It could occur, for example, in private medical practice if a consultant surgeon prescribed operations that weren't really necessary but brought in large fees.

However, it must be said that, for the most part, brokers' clients have been satisfied with the service they have received over many years.

The End of Single Capacity

We have seen, however, that the institutional users of the Stock Exchange were keen to do away with the fixed commission system because the brokers seemed to be getting money for a minimal service. The institutions needed little or no advice from stockbrokers as they had investment departments of their own; they were having to pay rather heavily for someone to go onto the Stock Exchange floor, do a deal, and follow up the paperwork. Other clients of the brokers, who did need a lot of advice, got more services for the same commission.

The argument for fixed minimum commissions was that, if they were not fixed, the rates would soon be reduced by competition and brokers would not find it worthwhile to act only as agents. They would have to do something else to make up their profits. Also, if they earn only a minute percentage on each deal, they may feel that spending time and resources scouring the market for the best terms would be a waste.

The Goodison-Parkinson pact of 1983 did not in itself specify the end of single capacity; but there was inherent in the ending of fixed commissions the likelihood that it *would* end.

If fixed commissions were abandoned, the brokers would compete to provide the cheapest service. They would want to supply their customers 'off the shelf' from their own stock, going short if necessary to absorb the jobber's turn and so make up for lost commission income. By the same token, they would want to buy up any shares they were offered to add to their stock. As brokers would then be performing a jobbing function, it seemed only fair that jobbers should have direct access to customers without having to use the broker.

A second nail in the coffin for single capacity was the restructuring of the gilt edged market (the market for UK government securities). The government was increasingly dissatisfied with the way this market was performing — it was just costing too much.

The government has to market its securities because it fails to collect in tax the full amount of its expenditure. It needs to approach the capital market to make up the difference. In the 1970s, public expenditure rose strongly, and the government had to sell a lot of gilts. But the market found it difficult to absorb all the new issues, and high rates of interest had to be offered in order to attract buyers. Because it really needed the money, however, the government did not worry too much about the cost of raising it.

The Conservative government of 1979 took a much more commercial attitude to the management of gilt sales. It wanted to increase competition amongst the jobbers who handled the business, partly to avoid unwelcome gilt 'strikes' when the market simply could not, or would not, absorb new issues. Such strikes push up interest rates, and can disrupt this vital form of public finance. By opening up the market to more dealers in gilts, particularly to large American companies which could retail gilts world-wide, the Bank of England now expects to ensure continuity in the market and a lower borrowing cost for the government. The government, too, felt that the fixed commissions charged by the gilt jobbers, on what was after all a high-volume business, were unreasonable. So, once again, exposing the stock market to greater competition could reduce the cost of each transaction.

It became clear to the jobbers that if they were to compete with the big American companies, they too would need to be big: hence their new enthusiasm for merging with cash-rich commercial banks. The significance for the stock market itself was that such competition was likely to spill over into the equity market. More competition must reduce commissions and, as we have seen, lower commissions pushed the brokers into market-making.

The New System — Competing Market Makers

The system that has evolved to replace single capacity is the Competing Market Maker system. Under this any member of the Stock Exchange is allowed to act both as a broker and as a jobber. Their funciton need not be specialised and they may be referred to as 'dealers'. Some firms will undoubtedly choose to pursue a single capacity, either from lack of opportunity — they cannot raise the finance to become market makers — or because they feel that their expertise is specific and still saleable even in the changing circumstances.

Every member will, however, have the option of becoming a registered market maker. If they do so, they will have to maintain two-way prices in the shares in which they have specialised; they will also be required to deal in a specified minimum number of shares. They will enjoy the same tax privileges as jobbers, and have access to the money broker should they need to borrow stock.

The Benefits of The New Arrangements

The chief advantage of the competing market maker system is that there will be more market makers. Competition between market makers specialising in any particular type of stock is likely to be fiercer. As for those types of stock which jobbers avoided under the old system, they are now more likely to find market makers to fill the niche. Thus, the gaps that were a disappointing aspect of the single capacity system should be closed. In short, the market should now become more competitive and a better mechanism for all firms to raise capital as and when they need it.

There are other advantages to the new system. It opens up the market to more members, some of whom can be based overseas. In fact, the presence of overseas dealers in the London Stock Exchange has been felt for a long time. After exchange controls went in 1979, many institutions invested overseas in order to widen the spread of their portfolios and to take advantage of the opportunities they saw. A large number of foreign banks had already located in London (often in order to trade in the eurobond and eurocurrency markets) and these were admirably placed to channel funds from UK institutions overseas. They were on the spot, but could provide good market intelligence about their own countries.

To respond to this challenge, the Stock Exchange began to allow dealings between its own members and 'Designated Dealers'. These were members of another stock exchange who were prepared to perform the same function for foreign shares as jobbers did in London, namely to maintain a continuous two-way price. As American brokers were prepared to pay a reciprocal commission to British brokers who put business their way, the flow of funds to the US (and to other countries) could be carried out profitably for all.

It was not long before members of the London Stock Exchange set up firms to trade on overseas stock exchanges; in effect the brokers then belonged to, and could trade on, two or more exchanges. This enabled them to operate pretty much under the rules of the foreign stock exchange. The implications were straightforward. If a big investment company wanted to buy shares in a large industrial enterprise, it could approach its broker. If the broker traded under UK rules, the customer would have to pay the fixed minimum commission. But if the shares were bought in the US market under US rules, a lower negotiated commission was possible. In consequence, fixed commissions for many such deals had become a cosmetic fiction long before the deregulation of the Stock Exchange was completed.

In 1983, the Stock Exchange formalised the procedure by defining an 'international dealer' as a subsidiary of a member firm, but one not subject to the minimum commission rules. With such arrangements, brokers can now maintain a 24-hour-a-day presence in the markets. When the London market closes in the early afternoon, dealing can begin in New York, and when New York closes at about midnight, the 'book' can be passed on to Tokyo until London opens again in the morning.

Another advantage of the competing market maker system is that it uses new technology: indeed, the success of the new system depends on it. The competing market-maker system needs many more market makers than the single capacity system and, if dealers are to find the best price they can, they will need to have access to information about all the market makers' quotations.

Previously, when the jobbers were few in number, a quick walk around the Exchange floor would tell the experienced dealer all there was to know. Now he must scan a VDU to find the best prices among an enlarged number of competing market makers. This has the advantage that members of the Stock Exchange will be on the same footing wherever they are. From one point of view at least, location outside London — be it in Harrogate or Hanover — need not be a handicap.

SEAQ will provide the heart of the new arrangements, with a wider participation than has been possible before; but it is unlikely to remove the need for the Stock Exchange floor altogether. Dealers will still want to get a personal feel of the market and SEAQ is unlikely to be seen as an adequate substitute for face-to-face interaction, at least at present. It remains to be seen how many shares will be traded on the floor and how many 'upstairs' via SEAQ. Very large transactions in blue chip stocks between big corporations will probably happen upstairs, as will very small ones. But most of the dealing in the shares of medium-sized companies is likely to remain on the floor.

. . . And The Costs

The ending of fixed commissions has led inevitably, it seems, to the formation of new, larger financial conglomerates; they can make markets in an environment where, to rely on commission income alone would mean lower profits.

It is within these large conglomerates that conflicts of interest are most likely to arise, and these conflicts of interest may reduce the value of the market to its users. Suppose a merchant bank, advising a client in a take-over, is merged with a stockbroker, one of whose clients is a big investment company which owns a substantial block of shares in the 'victim' of the take-over. The merchant bank division wants to promote the merger and tries to persuade shareholders to sell out. If it has a 'friend at court' who is also pushing for the merger, it is more likely to succeed. The stockbroking division is potentially such a friend; the advice it would give under these circumstances may not truly reflect the best interests of the investment company.

The City purports not to be too worried by this scenario, as it maintains that 'Chinese walls' will operate effectively: that is, there are well understood codes of practice under which investment advisers, for example, do not discuss sensitive matters with their colleagues specialising in take-overs. To make those invisible walls more effective, many companies have physically separated their various arms by putting them in different buildings, or at least on different floors.

There is both sense and self-interest in these Chinese walls. If clients feel that they have been given bad advice, or that their secrets are likely to be leaked for the benefit of others, they will soon take their business elsewhere.

Another possible disadvantage of the new arrangements is that the market itself might change for the worse. When a jobber does business he is not doing it with his competitors. Like any wholesaler, he wants a high volume of trade on which he can make his margin. In order to do business, he may quote a closer price or be prepared to deal in a larger volume so as to keep a customer for the future than would be his inclination otherwise. Market makers in the new system, on the other hand, are in direct competition with each other. There is no incentive for them to offer close prices or high volumes if they don't wish to do so.

Competing market makers play a zero sum game: if one gains, the other must lose because they are both dealing on their own behalf. In a single capacity system, however, both brokers and jobbers can gain if the volume of business is high enough, and so both have an interest in ensuring that it is so. As neither of them takes a long term position in the market, they can both do well whichever way prices move. This makes for orderly markets and gentlemanly conduct. Some observers fear that the competing marketeers will wheel and deal in such a way as to disrupt the smooth running of the market.

The New Market In Gilts

In order to solve its two-fold problem with the gilt edged market, namely the high cost of operating the market and the occasional gilt strike, the government has developed a new structure for the market in its securities. Participants in this market will fall into three broad categories.

The first are the market makers who will undertake to quote two-way prices continuously on a wide variety of securities. The firms most likely to do this are the old stock jobbers with their new partners, the large US primary dealers in treasury stock, and stockbrokers who feel that they have good outlets for the securities they purchase.

The risks in dealing in gilts are quite considerable. Changes in the interest rate, the exchange rate, the price of oil, wars and sundry items of economic news from both the US and the UK can all affect prices. Since the market is competitive, and prices close, market makers are likely to do business between themselves in order to reduce an exposed position. The aim of the market maker is to make sure his portfolio is the right shape (ratio of long to short government debt) and the right way (not over-exposed to changes in interest rates).

The second category of dealers in the gilt edged market is the inter-dealer broker (IDB); he acts as an intermediary who can arrange sales and purchases between the market makers. This is a useful function as market makers are naturally anxious that their competitors should not know the moves they are making in the market; the IDBs guarantee anonymity. The IDBs can be used to keep the market makers in shape and the right way.

The third category of participant is the stock market money broker. He continues his role as a lender of money to those market makers who are long, and a lender of stock to those who are short.

Uncertain future for the floor: too crowded with new dealers — or redundant?

Presiding over them all will be the government broker whose job it is to ensure that the government gets what it wants from the market. He will need to maintain contact with the new market makers who have expressed their desire to join the market. It is likely, though, that within a few years some of them will find the competition too tough, and drop out. The government broker's prime aim is to sell stock, though he may also buy some if he feels that the market lacks liquidity.

Conclusion

The Big Bang does not necessarily mean the end of single capacity firms. Such firms will still exist, marketing their specialised services. Some will just provide a cheap brokerage service for investors who don't want advice or research facilities from their broker. Others will find a niche for themselves in the provinces, providing facilities for the retail market. SEAQ can only improve the quality of their services. Banks, building societies and even large retail stores may find their way into this end of the market and use their membership of the Exchange to compete with the old guard of provincial brokers. Which institutions our new share-owning democracy will choose to patronise remains uncertain.

Some firms will become market makers, taking a position in some specific sector of the market. American experience of deregulation suggests that, after an initial honeymoon period, many of the market makers fail or need to merge to achieve the size needed to cope with the risks of taking positions. In Britain, the realignment has been happening before the Big Bang, and this may result in a more stable evolution.

In the past, membership of the London Stock Exchange has tended to be individual and the individuals have come from partnerships within the UK; but the future is likely to see more corporations sponsoring membership and more overseas participants.

Dealing itself is likely to be more vigorous than in the past, at least in some sectors of the market, and some dealing, namely in gilts and blue chip securities, will be done largely over the telephone on the basis of SEAQ information. Other securities, however, are still likely to be traded on the Stock Exchange floor.

The combination of technology and competition may have made the Big Bang inevitable, but they also make its outcome very uncertain as far as the Stock Exchange is concerned.

16
The Lloyd's Insurance Market

It is not the Big Bang itself which is causing the present upheavals in the Lloyd's insurance market. Rather it is underlying changes of which the Big Bang itself is a symptom.

Traditionally, Lloyd's has been a market in which the 'names' — members considered to have enough personal wealth to carry the risks on the insurance market — arrange for a small group of professional managers to accept insurance risks on their behalf. These managers are normally referred to as underwriters, though, more properly, it is the names themselves that underwrite the risk — that is, they are responsible for them. Insurance brokers approach the underwriters on the floor of Lloyd's and introduce business to them. The underwriters then accept the business or not, depending on whether they feel that the premium offered will compensate their syndicate for the risks of the business proposed.

The system depends on two factors for its success. First, the names must be able to put together, singly or as a syndicate, enough capital to underwrite the risks put forward by the brokers. Second, the professional managers must be competent to judge risks correctly so that the market rewards investors — who will thus continue to come forward — as well as providing a fair service for its clients. In both these respects, doubt has been cast on Lloyd's ability to dominate the insurance market as it once did.

The market began when the scale of business activity, and therefore of the risks that were being underwritten, were much smaller than they are today. The assets insured now are worth billions rather than millions. Furthermore, since the market is an international one, all the risks of fluctuating interest and exchange rates make the assessment of risk that much harder. In the past Lloyd's was chiefly concerned with providing a service for British manufacturing and commercial activity, for the most part marine insurance. The bulk of the business now is *non*-marine insurance sold largely to the Japanese and American markets. As the price of the Yen and the dollar change, so does the value of the premium become more uncertain, as does the sterling value of the risk.

Lloyd's new building: the Underwriting Room viewed from Gallery Four.

The obvious response is to open the market to a greater number of names; larger risks can be borne by a correspondingly larger number of people. But this all makes the market a harder place to control. In effect, the names become further divorced from the management of the business they do, and forced to rely more and more on the underwriters. Obviously, if the underwriters are providing bad intermediation between the names and their customers, either names or customers will eventually stop coming forward to deal.

Recently, some of the names have felt that the quality of the service given by their underwriters has left a lot to be desired; there have even been allegations of malpractice. In particular, the formation of 'baby' syndicates, where a group of underwriters take the most profitable business for themselves rather than pass it on to the names, has been criticised. Similarly, some rather dubious techniques for avoiding tax liability have also been called into question.

The Lloyd's Act of 1982 allows Lloyd's to regulate itself and to provide whatever discipline is needed to conduct the market fairly and professionally, but there is some doubt as to whether this system should be allowed to continue. It is now thought that there is a potential conflict of interest between the underwriters' wish to do business on their own behalf, and their ability to provide an impartial management service for the names. In essence, what is being questioned is a dual capacity system — just when the Stock Exchange is about to abandon its own single capacity trading in favour of dual capacity. The Department of Trade and Industry has set up an enquiry into the regulation of the Lloyd's market and its findings are likely to determine whether Lloyd's can still regulate itself or whether it will come under legislation in the Financial Services Bill, along with other self-regulating markets in the City.

The outcome of this issue has wider ramifications than those for the insurance market alone. Underwriters not only collect up huge sums of money in premiums, they also invest them, helped by almost every kind of financial intermediary. The banks, the merchant banks, the stockbrokers, and so on, all have a common interest in the success of the insurance market.

17
Financial Futures

A financial futures contract is an agreement to buy or sell a specific financial instrument at an agreed price and date in the future. Financial futures enable investors to hedge (insure) against uncertainties about the future performance of almost any financial instrument.

Similar facilities have existed in commodity markets for a long time. A manufacturer who uses a lot of copper, for example, may want to secure his supply in the future at a fixed price. He can go to the futures market and negotiate a deal whereby he promises to accept delivery at a specified date in the future of a specified quantity of copper, and to pay an agreed price. On that date the dealer with whom he made this futures contract must go to the 'spot' market (i.e. the market for immediate delivery) and buy the quantity of copper he has agreed to supply and deliver it to the manufacturer. If the spot price is *less* than the futures contract price, then the dealer has made a gain on the transaction at the expense of the manufacturer. But the manufacturer has at least been certain that the copper would be delivered at the right time at a certain price.

Any loss the manufacturer makes on such deals must be regarded as the premium he has to pay for such assurance. There is always the possibility, too, that the spot price may be *above* the future contract price. If so, the manufacturer has not only insured himself against an adverse price movement, he will have bought his copper more cheaply as a result of his foresight in trading on the futures market.

There is another alternative open to the manufacturer. Rather than contracting to buy copper on some future date, he can buy an 'option to buy'. To obtain this option, he will have to pay a premium; but having done so, he can then wait and see what happens to the spot price. If it falls below the option price, then he can allow his option to lapse and simply buy what he needs in the spot market. If, on the other hand, the spot price rises above the traded option price, then he will obviously claim his option to buy supplies at less than the current market price. In this way commodity futures and options markets help people to hedge against future uncertainties and 'bet' on future price movements in the hope of making a capital gain.

The floor of the London International Financial Futures Exchange will play a key role in the new City.

Financial futures markets grew out of the commodity markets. The raw materials in some businesses are far less tangible than copper, or indeed than any other physical commodity. The raw material for financial institutions are bonds, currencies, shares, gilts and so on. Just as a manufacturer may need copper to do the business he does, so a bank may need gilt edged securities. In order to secure these at a definite price, they use the financial futures market. What is more, if in one part of its business a financial conglomerate is becoming rather exposed to (say) falls in the rate of interest in the UK, then it can hedge itself in the financial futures market. The market has proved to be a useful exchange.

Like the Big Bang itself, the establishment of LIFFE (the London International Futures Exchange) is a symptom of the underlying changes in the financial markets wrought by technology, innovation and government activity. When interest rates, exchange rates, commodity prices and stock indices began to fluctuate widely, investors sought to hedge against such changes. A financial futures market was quickly set up in Chicago to enable them to do this, and dealers in financial futures soon found that dealing on their own account rather than just as agents for the hedgers could be very profitable. The idea caught on rapidly in London, which was and remains the leading financial centre for dealing in eurocurrencies and bonds, foreign exchange and sterling denominated interest-bearing paper. These markets were all volatile and LIFFE could therefore provide a useful service. The fact that London lies in a convenient time-zone between Tokyo and New York, allowing dealing for 24 hours a day, was another important factor. The market now trades in US treasury bonds, interest rate futures (3-month eurodollar and 3-month sterling), currency futures and stock index futures. As more and more market makers appear in the post-Big Bang City, LIFFE can look forward to booming business as the new dealers seek to offset the risks involved in taking positions in the market.

18
The Commodity Markets

If it is possible to generalise at all about City markets today, then we can say they are all, in some measure, moving away from their original purpose. Much of the trade done in the markets is quite unconnected to any real flow of goods and services, and is increasingly speculative. Buying and selling have become ends in themselves rather than a means to an end.

We can also say that all markets are becoming ever harder to regulate as the size of their business grows and dwarfs the resources of the regulatory authorities. A third and closely related observation would be that these markets also tend to become more complex as new products or ways of doing business are invented that only insiders can really understand. Recent events in the London Metal Exchange have shown that commodity markets are far from immune from these trends.

The London Metal Exchange has traditionally been the pre-eminent market for dealing in non-precious metals. The prices of these metals are fixed each day during separate auction sessions, attended by the 24 members who buy and sell directly. The market is self-regulated and has shown itself to be an effective intermediary. As the market was small, it was possible to know all the dealers within it personally and so considerable trust was built up.

This trust was shattered late in 1985 when one of the primary dealers in tin, the International Tin Council (ITC) declared itself unable to continue trading. The ITC was established by the big tin producers and its job was to intervene in tin markets to limit fluctuations in tin prices. This was done by maintaining a buffer stock from which tin could be sold when it was scarce and the price was rising. If prices were falling, the ITC could buy and add to its buffer stock.

Earlier in 1985, supplies of tin had outstripped demand and there was selling pressure on the spot market. In the futures market, dealers began to sell short in anticipation of a fall in price. The ITC intervened and extended itself to the full, obtaining credit not just from its bankers but from other dealers in the LME. It was confident in the belief that its sponsors would provide the funds needed to honour its commitments. But the Buffer Stock managers were mistaken: no further funds were forthcoming.

When the collapse came, it became clear that the price of tin was going to fall sharply, leaving the ITC with a vast stock on which it was going to make a huge capital loss. It owed money to banks and to other dealers, and this caused ripples of anxiety in the market as each dealer began to wonder whether other dealers could honour contracts they had made. For a time, it looked as though the collapse of the ITC would cause other dealers to collapse and create so much uncertainty as to make the continuation of dealing in the traditional way impossible.

There are a number of lessons to be learned from the experience of the LME which throw some light on how markets behave in general. The sponsors of the ITC, who were mostly the governments of the big tin producing countries, failed to respond immediately to the appeals of the LME that they should honour the debts of the organisation they had set up. They argued that the ITC was a limited liability company, and so they expected their liability to be limited. In short, they showed themselves to be impervious to the old-style City discipline of appeals to common decency or fair play reinforced by the threat of ostracism.

The existing method of market regulation depended upon mutual trust between dealers, and hence upon confidence in each other's ability to honour contracts. It failed to work when an 'outsider' (or its representative) began to deal. Needless to say, the whole experience underlined what was already known all too well: in small markets with large dealers, the collapse of one dealer is apt to bring down others. Today, world capital markets can hardly be called small; but, as we have seen, the tendancy is for dealers in these markets to grow bigger and bigger. The collapse of even one large financial institution anywhere in the world is bound to affect others everywhere, with as yet incalculable consequences for the future.

Part Four
The Human Dimension

19 The Outlook for Stockbrokers' Private Clients

The private clients of the stockbrokers have had rather a bad deal in recent years. As tax changes encouraged savers to use insurance companies and pension funds as a channel for their savings, direct investment on the Stock Exchange by individuals became a minority business. Stockbrokers soon found that providing a bulk buying/selling service for institutions involved lower overhead costs than those incurred in acting for hundreds of small investors. The fixed commission system offered no incentive to provide a personal (and more costly service) for individuals.

The ending of fixed commissions, and the likelihood that the big institutions would use their muscle to force down commission rates, caused brokers to look again at private clients' business. Indeed, the smaller firms of stockbrokers (those lacking the capital to become market makers) will find the commission on institutional business — even if they can get it — so small as to make their very survival depend on how many private clients they can keep.

Other changes seem to favour small investors on the Stock Exchange as well. The current thrust of government legislation is to encourage share ownership. The stamp duty on share dealing may well be further reduced or abolished: it is a disincentive to investors. Furthermore, improvements in technology make it cheaper for brokers to deal in relatively small quantities of shares. The paperwork can be automated so that a 'personal' service can be provided with fewer skilled (and expensive) personnel.

Finally, the private investor is likely to be offered stockbroking services by a wide array of different financial institutions. Stockbrokers will be joined by commercial banks, building societies and perhaps even retail department stores in chasing his business. The people who handle his investments will become less remote, probably even having high street branches. They will be more welcoming and flexible since the commission that he is willing to pay compares more and more favourably with what can be earned on institutional business.

Personal tax reform may also create a new generation of investors on the Stock Exchange. Lower rates of tax for high income earners, and other measures which make capital accumulation easier, will provide greater scope for direct investment.

20
The Outlook for City Employees

When the supply of cabbages falls short of demand, the price will be bid up in a free market. Skills are not unlike cabbages in this respect, which explains the remarkable escalation of City salaries that has occurred over the past few years. Pay in the City has always been higher than in other sectors of the British economy, but the tendency recently has been for the gap to widen even further.

The reasons for this can be readily identified. First, the Big Bang has created an almost universal demand for market making skills. The abolition of fixed commissions, and the new competing market maker system, has meant that more institutions than ever before want to assemble teams of dealers able to take a position in the market profitably. Such people are in scarce supply; the large financial conglomerates have therefore had to pay higher salaries to entice individuals, and sometimes whole teams, away from their existing employers.

The second factor behind rising City salaries is that, with deregulation and the growth of financial markets generally, more firms (foreign investment banks and Japanese securities houses in particular) have wanted to set up subsidiaries or branches in the UK. They, too, have swelled the numbers of those greedy for talent.

A third and associated reason for the rise in City salaries is the internationalisation of the market place. American experts who come to work in the City of London will not take a drop in salary simply because they are moving from a high wage to a low wage economy. They therefore import high wages which are then transmitted to the domestic economy by individuals comparing salaries and questioning differentials.

Interestingly, the City is producing not just high salary earners but individuals able to accumulate capital as well. The 'Golden Hello' (an enticement paid upon recruitment) and the many bonuses and commissions paid on business successfully completed, is in part an explanation of this. So is the merger mania of the past few years during which huge sums have been paid, for example, to partners in firms of stockbrokers for their interest in the business. Finally, when people work in a market where prices change rapidly, the chance of making speculative gains always exists. The more volatile the market, the more the risk, and thus the greater the potential gain — or loss. In recent years, speculators have been able to find markets volatile enough to enable them to build capital quickly.

The important question is: where will it all end? Even the government, keen to promote the financial services sector to make up for the decline in manufacturing, is becoming embarrassed by the widening salary gap which draws the most talented graduates into the City. However, any tax designed specifically to reduce this imbalance is likely to cost more to collect than it yields, and it would also be fraught with political difficulties.

City salaries are unlikely to fall but when a post-Big Bang stasis is reached, and as the supply of people with the necessary skills increases, they may grow less rapidly. Much of the reorganisation of the past three years is evidence of the banks' and brokers' belief that commissions will be lower in future and that costs will have to be pruned. As people are the main current costs for most City institutions, they may have to be pruned as well. This factor, combined with the tendency to pay a large proportion of salary in the form of bonus, plus the volatility of the market, means that salaries are probably going to fluctuate widely and that job security will be low. It is not difficult to foresee a situation in which the big financial institutions would shed employees in droves. A low volume of business in any particular market, or an inability to cope with the competition, or even the re-establishment of exchange controls, could each cause firms to shut down whole departments. Indeed, many observers think that after a few years, the new financial conglomerates will move back to specialising in what they do best rather than providing a one-stop supermarket service. In this case they will require a second shake-up in the course of which they will shed many of the people they are now so anxious to recruit.

The City will certainly continue to be a place where the talented and those who possess valuable skills will be uniquely able to earn high incomes and build capital. But, in the future, they will do so in a rather uncertain environment and, for the unsuccessful, a hostile one. Some may find that, having been made redundant at thirty, they are unemployable in the City and have no experience of anything else. Others will find that by the same age they will be able to retire comfortably.

Part Five
Regulation —
The Government's Dilemma

21
Insular Clannish & Small: How the City Has Not Coped

In spite of the enormous sums handled, a remarkable feature of the City is its smallness, a fact emphasised by the term the 'square mile'. This smallness fosters the traditional ideals of personal contact, of being within easy walking distance of everyone you need to deal with. At the same time, however, it reinforces the influence of the old school tie; this inevitably exerts great power in a society where so many decision-makers come from a narrow social background dominated by the great independent schools like Eton and Harrow. Smallness and intimacy may give more substance to such worthy principles as 'my word is my bond', but they also make it easier for the system to succumb to three serious dangers: insularity, clannishness and inadequate capitalisation.

Insularity is the very opposite of the open-minded and thrusting internationalism needed if the City is to go on bridging the visible trade gap. Clannishness is a fertile breeding-ground for the germs of fraud and corruption which strike at the heart of a financial system. If they are allowed to gain a foothold, self-regulation becomes unworkable, scandals erupt, and credibility is destroyed. Inadequate capitalisation means, quite simply, you've got to be big if you are going to meet the needs of today's largest, most prestigeous clients. According to the *Economist*, in 1983 the total market value of Britain's six biggest publicly quoted merchant banks was less than £1 billion, while the American firm Merrill Lynch on its own was worth £2.7 billion. We have seen how the pursuit of size in response to market challenge has led to a veritable invasion of foreign financial institutions whose code of conduct is different from, and some would say worse than, that which has governed the City hitherto.

Even the alert intervention of the Bank of England has not guaranteed the standards of integrity and service needed. Regulation of professional practices has been a haphazard affair, administered by the practitioners themselves according to rules established over many years, often with little or no official intervention. The strictest external control has been maintained over the banking system, yet it still proved impossible to spot and forestall the Johnson Matthey crisis of the early 1980s, or the secondary banking crisis a decade earlier. Likewise, at Lloyd's, whose affairs have been internally regulated for over a century under statutory arrangements, there have been, as we have noted, conflicts of interest which have led to allegations of malpractice and even of corruption.

In the face of the much-publicised scandals it is important to keep a proper perspective. The sums of money being handled in the City are of truly staggering proportions; the number of people involved is relatively small; the opportunities for dishonesty and the temptations to take them can only be guessed at, but they must on occasion be colossal. It is therefore something of a marvel that the system has worked so well for so long. It can only be put down to the real personal integrity of the overwhelming majority of City people. A battalion of Solomons could not establish a set of rules sufficiently wise and comprehensive to prevent fraud and corruption on a massive scale if the practitioners themselves generally lacked this honesty.

Regulation is not easy. In the first place, whatever rules are invented there will always be an incentive to evade such rules. Indeed, the best minds in the country will often be deployed to see how this can be done. Regulation must be firm against the dishonest or imprudent, but flexible enough to foster new ideas and the generation of new products. It must protect the investor, but not stultify the market. Regulation must also be enforceable. If it limits a practice in one market only to drive it overseas to less well regulated shores, then little will have been achieved.

As markets become international, regulation will need to be coordinated across national frontiers. Certainly the market in foreign exchange now has an international dynamic; it is clear that intervention in support of a currency by one nation is unlikely to deter dealers if they are mounting a serious assault on that currency. The balances of foreign exchange available even to a central bank are now small in comparison to the world-wide money flows of the international banking system. To support a currency today, coordinated action by *all* cental banks is necessary and even this is risky if the timing is wrong. If currency dealers all feel that the price of sterling will fall, (as they did in the winter of 1985), it *will* fall, as they all dump sterling on the market to avoid a capital loss.

Such movements tend to be self-reinforcing. With modern technology, the ripple effect, whereby one dealer's expectations are quickly passed on to another, can have devastating results — as the British government learned when the pound approached parity with the American dollar in 1985. The remorseless downward pressure was unstoppable until the dealers themselves began to doubt the future trend. At that stage intervention could work; before, the government could only stand helplessly by and wait.

The market for foreign exchange is perhaps the most technologically advanced in the world. It is easy to see how expectations about future price movements are flashed about the world on VDUs and telephone lines. However, the market for securities is not far behind. Dealers are now seeing themselves not so much as members of the New York or London Stock Exchange but as members of a world exchange who just happen to be located in those capitals. Price movements in one market will be reflected simultaneously in others and, more significantly, expectations of *future* price movements will flash from one exchange to the other with potentially disastrous effects. The Wall Street Crash of 1929 had an indirect effect on economies world-wide, as American business faltered, and an important market for other countries' exports dried up. A Wall Street Crash of 1989, if there should be one, will shake every financial capital in the world to its foundations.

The new technology of the dealing room has another important effect, and one which makes regulation even more important. Since it provides a wider spectrum of dealers with greater and faster information than ever before, it means that if one institution finds a lucrative niche in the market, others will quickly discover it too. We have already seen how the syndicated lending of recycled petrocurrency to the developing countries became the craze of the 1970s. It was not just one bank that plunged into this business but, as the psychology of stampede took over, hundreds followed suit. In the event of a default, the disaster will not be local to just one bank, but a widespread collapse. Moreover, if financial institutions have to be big in order to survive, this concentration suggests that the failure of even one bank will have considerable impact on the financial community as a whole.

Recently, there have been two conspicuous failures—JMB in the UK and Continental Illinois in the US. Both ran into difficulties because they lent unwisely to clients who were eventually unable to repay. The authorities have managed to limit the damage but only by direct and visible intervention. Intervention after the event is much less satisfactory than stricter regulation of banking practice continuously. Only this can really ensure that the system never fails, and that investors and depositors are saved from an agony of decision-making to find a safe place for their savings. These failures occurred because of bad banking management and so were confined to the banks in question. But if the banks stampede to lend to one particular industry or country, and that industry or country betrays their optimism, the entire system could collapse.

The new technology allows crowd behaviour in the financial community. Indeed, it encourages it. Who wants to be left behind when prices are rising, or hold securities whilst they are falling? Markets can overshoot, overreacting to good or bad news. If this happens, the market is no longer introducing buyers and sellers seeking a fair market price for assets with some real worth. Instead there is a struggle to buy and sell bits of paper speculatively in such a way that their price completely fails to represent the value of their related real assets.

When this happened in the past, and securities were traded only on the Stock Exchange, the authorities could limit panic by shutting down the physical market place; that removed the only forum in which panic could be communicated. If the dealers did not meet each other, they could hardly pass on each others' anxieties. But locking the doors today has less effect; so much dealing is done off the floor. Indeed, there *is* no floor for trading many of today's new financial instruments. The authorities may be forced in the future to shut down whole telecommunications networks — a much trickier thing to achieve. Here again, international cooperation will be required, but since financial centres are competing with each other in an industry essential to their economic welfare, this might prove difficult. After all, regulation in New York which drives business to London is potentially good for Britain: the decline in our manufacturing has made the rise of the financial sector look very much like a life-raft.

22
The New System of Regulation

The Financial Services Bill, which seeks to provide a new framework for the regulation of financial institutions, tries to keep the best of the old wherever possible. The government clearly feels that the system of self-regulation which has endured so long has the merit of letting those who know the business best be the watchdogs. It also puts most of the cost of supervision onto the industry itself.

However, it is quite clear that as the City becomes a more open market, it will attract institutions and individuals less sympathetic to the old controls of nods and winks from the financial authorities. What is proposed, therefore, is a system of self-regulatory bodies specialised by function, operating with a statutory framework. Ultimate responsibility for the success of the City will lie with the Department of Trade and Industry (DTI) which will appoint a Securities and Investment Board (SIB). This will directly oversee the work of the Self Regulatory Organisations (SRO), and have the power to overide their decisions. The diagram below shows how the formal organisation might look:

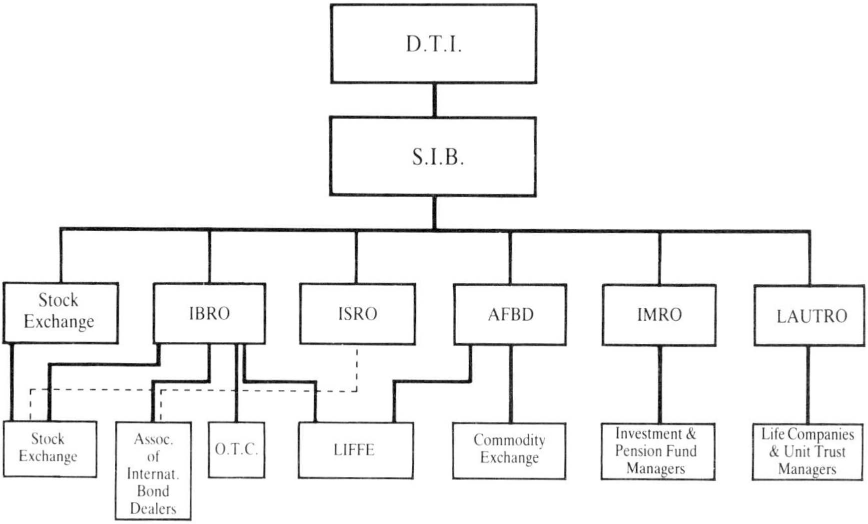

IBRO (Investment Brokers and Dealers Regulatory Organisations): This is a merger of NASDIM (National Association of Securities Dealers and Investment Managers) and LUTIRO (Life and Unit Trust Intermediaries Organisation). The aim is to ensure that one set of rules holds for all firms doing the same kind of business and that no firm has to report to two organisations for doing the same business. IBRO is concerned with all firms dealing in securities, eurobonds, futures, and options.

Stock Exchange: This regulates all dealers who operate on the domestic stock market.

AFBD (Association of Futures Brokers and Dealers): This is concerned with dealers on LIFFE (*London International Financial Futures Exchange*).

IMRO (Investment Managers Regulatory Organisation): Concerned with any institution that provides investment management services as well as the trustees of pension funds.

LAUTRO (Life Assurance and Unit Trust Regulatory Organisation): Concerned with firms and individuals marketing unit trust and insurance linked investments.

Problems of Regulation

The first problem the Government has faced in its attempt to restructure City regulation has been a series of protests from the SROs. These have been concerned that, if the present proposals go ahead as planned, they are liable to claims for damages both from member organisations and from investors. If one of the SROs suspends a financial institution from dealing in the market, and is later found to have acted unjustly, then the institution can sue for damages for loss of both business and reputation. Either one of these could result in an enormous settlement against the SRO. As the market becomes more international, the American penchant for litigation may well spread to the City; the SROs are concerned lest the threat of law suits by rich corporations will discourage disciplinary action. In America the regulatory bodies have immunity from claims for damages. Many observers think that, without such immunity, the SROs may be inoperable in the UK.

The second problem is what to do when conflicts of interest arise within one of the big financial conglomerates? If there is a corporate finance division, a market making brokerage, and an investment management division within one enterprise, there will be times when the conflict of interest is acute.

The Bank of England, the government's agent in the City, stands at the heart of the Square Mile.

The new Financial Services Bill is based on the premise that Chinese walls really can work, and that the conglomerates will obey those regulations forbidding insider trading. As already argued, this is not as naive as it may seem, as it is in the conglomerate's interest to maintain a good reputation for all the services it provides. Now that individual employees are very mobile between different companies, leaks in the Chinese walls will soon become common knowledge.

To cope with the problem of insider trading the new Bill sets out two procedures. First, it requires that, in drawing up their rule-book, the SROs should do their utmost to build leak-proof Chinese Walls. Second, it states that financial institutions must disclose to the client any interest which may cause a conflict. Given such knowledge, the clients can then decide whether that institution will act in their best interest, or whether they should look elsewhere. It is too early to say how successful all this will be in eliminating insider trading, but the financial institutions do seem to be making an effort to establish Chinese walls both by the physical separation of different departments, and by making rules of procedure which provide safeguards.

Cynical observers might wonder whether Chinese Walls don't conflict with some, at least, of the objectives which led to the formation of the conglomerates in the first place — for instance, the pooling of the skills of different firms.

Conclusion

The spectacular failure of the South Seas Company so shocked the legislators of the eighteenth century that they passed a law which effectively outlawed the formation of joint stock companies for the next hundred years. No doubt, when that Act was repealed, there were some who were anxious lest the new joint stock companies should go the same way as the South Seas Company. On balance they were wrong. of course, there have been failures and these have damaged the economy. But, on the whole, the joint stock system has lasted well and has shown itself to be a flexible and useful means of arranging business affairs.

What we are experiencing now is something like the repeal of the Bubble Act. Governments world-wide are allowing changes to business practices that have for many years either saved us from financial disaster or hindered legitimate business activity — depending, of course, on your point of view.

Which is it? So far, experience suggests that, until recently, our financial institutions have been operating in a restrictive environment which has prevented them from giving the best service and the keenest prices to their customers, and which has failed to encourage innovation. Only when the eurobond and eurocurrency markets got going, entirely unregulated, did financiers really begin to see the limitations of the old system.

Technology permitted them to bypass a number of these regulations; the threat of relocation to other, more tolerant, financial capitals persuaded governments of the virtue of bowing to the inevitable. If the markets could not be controlled because they were off-shore or international, then most governments decided it was better to keep them in the traditional financial capitals where there was a chance of getting at least some compliance. It takes a very tough government indeed to discourage a growth sector at a time when others are in recession.

So far we have seen the Americans weather their own deregulation successfully. Of course, there have been structural changes in the US financial services industry — a tendency towards concentration and diversification, for example. But the system itself has survived to fight another day (even if not all the individual firms and their employees have). If anything, the market seems to be more responsive to the needs of investors and borrowers who can bask in the sunshine of competition for their business. If there has been a cost, it has been the cost of failing financial institutions in the wake of the deregulation; these are legitimate casualties. In London, the adjustment so far has been quite painless. As firms merge to position themselves for the post Big Bang world, money is made and salaries increase. The redundant few can often tell stories of gaining both a capital sum as a pay-off from their previous employer and a Golden Hello and a higher salary from the next.

The story is not over, however. In London the final outcome of the Big Bang remains to be seen. How the new UK financial conglomerates will weather competition from the foreign banks and securities houses is anyone's guess; but it would be remarkable if they all managed to survive and flourish. There will surely be some noteworthy casualties.

There is an even more serious point. Unfettered international competition and the new technology in the financial services market has benefited almost everyone — so far. But how far is 'so far'?

There is nothing unique in free markets which makes for the best possible outcome. Indeed, history would suggest the opposite. It is no accident that financial institutions have been subject to strict regulation throughout the centuries. After all, what they supply is essential, and all the evidence suggests that, when left to their own devices, they do *not* arrange their affairs in the most productive way, or in the way most likely to help the economy.

After the South Seas Company was floated there was a period when everyone was better off, whether they had sold the stock, or bought it. But this short honeymoon was soon to end, not just in a financial disaster for the company and its supporters, but in the abolition of the entire joint stock system.

Economies in the eighteenth century were less tightly knit than they are now. The South Seas disaster felt bad at the time but it was limited in impact. In other parts of Britain and in other sectors of the economy, business went on much as before. Money could still be used to buy goods and services, and trade continued.

The absence of spill-over effects of a disaster depends on each part of the financial system being more or less independent of the others. This situation can hardly be said to exist today. In the London Metal Exchange, the failure of one dealer created difficulties, not just in the tin market but in the metal market as a whole. The affairs of the dealers were so inextricably intertwined that the failure of one threatened to bring down others and, ultimately, the entire market.

When markets perform their simplest function, which is to put buyers of a product that has some real worth in touch with sellers, then not much can go wrong. Crops may fail, demand may contract, prices soar or plummet, but the discomfort is likely to be short-lived. If people still want the product, and others are willing to supply it, then the market will overcome such distortions in the long run.

But once the markets become an end in themselves, and when financial institutions do too much incestuous business with each other rather than with the general public, things can go seriously wrong.

The commercial banks, for instance, operate in the market for personal finance. If they borrow from and lend to their customers and do nothing else, then the business is as good as the decisions the banks take about who is creditworthy, what rates of interest to pay depositors, and so on. If, on the other hand, the banks begin to borrow or lend to other financial institutions, then the success of the business depends not just on the managers of the banks themselves, but on the management of the other financial institutions.

There is an old story that says that if you owe the bank £5 and you cannot pay, you have a problem; but if you owe the bank £5m and cannot pay, then the bank has a problem. This is all very true. But if one bank owes another bank £50m and cannot pay, then we *all* have a problem.

Financial institutions do, of course, lend to each other. Indeed, the interbank market exists solely for this purpose and is often cited as a safety net which prevents bank failures. When one bank runs short of cash because of heavy withdrawals, it can borrow on the interbank market until it has traded out of its difficulties. If this happens then lending between institutions clearly allows for more certain banking and is therefore a good thing. However, there is an awful tendency for the interbank market to dry up in the face of those who need it most. When Continental Illinois needed to borrow to cover withdrawals, their credit rating was slashed by other banks who refused to lend.

The Continental Illinois problem was finally solved by almost unlimited intervention by the US monetary authorities, which prevented successive failures. But it was not long before another big American bank came under pressure from anxious depositors. It is not hard to imagine a situation in which even the action of a central bank will prove ineffective. If financial institutions lend too much of their assets to each other, and one fails, that failure can quickly spread like an infection to others. If depositors see several institutions in trouble they may start such a rush of withdrawals that nothing could stop it, nor the inevitable collapse of the entire monetary system that would follow.

It is to government that we must look to ensure that such things never happen. In the past strict regulation has ensured that each part of the financial system is able to survive. If every brick in the financial edifice is sound, and remains in place, there is a good chance that the edifice will remain standing.

The edifice is now getting very big and complicated. Individual countries naturally try to insulate their own institutions from world market forces to avoid importing disaster, but it can no longer be done completely. New technology and freedom from exchange controls have prevented them from doing so. For regulation to succeed, it will surely have to be coordinated internationally.

Financial institutions are not only becoming more interdependent, they are also seeking to diversify into new markets in which they have little experience. Commercial banks are drumming up international securities business and are hoisting their flags over conglomerates who will completely redefine what banks do. In these unfamiliar and stormy waters there must be a chance at least that some will sink. If they do, there is bound to be some adverse knock-on effect for their traditional customers. If a bank conspicuously loses out in the securities markets then its customers may wish to withdraw their savings — just in case.

Commercial banks are not the only financial institutions getting into deeper waters. Building societies are becoming like banks, investment banks are becoming like building societies, unit trusts are performing a life assurance role, and so on.

The potential benefits on the other hand are considerable. When markets are free and buyers are well informed, those buyers support the firms which provide the best service at the best price. Others will have to respond or quit the market. The result should be wider choice, lower costs and better products.

Costs, however, there most certainly are, though they exist in a form that is neither immediate nor straightforward. If the changes in financial markets, which have culminated in the Big Bang and all that it implies, have made regulation more difficult and less certain, then we are in greater jeopardy from fraud and malpractice; and, if the very worst happened, there would be a complete failure of the financial system world wide. We must all hope and trust that the Big Bang will not end in a whimper.

Appendix

The following is a list of some of the important representative City Institutions.

Merchant Banks, Investment Banks, etc.

Accepting Houses Committee, Granite House, 101 Cannon Street, London EC4N 5BA.

Association of International Bond Dealers, International House, St. Katharines Way, London E1 9UN.

Issuing Houses Association, Granite House, 101 Cannon Street, London EC4N 5BA.

Commercial Banks

Association of Consortium Banks, Scandinavia House, 2-4 Cannon Street, London EC4M 6XX.

British Bankers Association, 10 Lombard Street, London EC3V 9AR.

Banking Information Service, 10 Lombard Street, London EC3V 9AR.

International C.D. Market Association, c/o Drexel Burnham Lambert Inc, 100 Old Broad Street, London EC2N 1BE.

Stock Market

Association of Stock and Share Dealers, 165 Queen Victoria Street, London EC4V 4DD.

Automated Real Time Investment Exchange Ltd, Ibex House, 42-47 Minories, London EC3N 1EU.

British Security Industry Association, 21 Whitefriars Street, London EC4Y 8AL.

Stock Exchange, London EC2N 1HP.

United Kingdom Association of New York Stock Exchange Members, c/o Shearson Lehman International Ltd, Peninsular House, 24 Monument Street, London EC3R 8AJ.

United Kingdom Association of Tokyo Stock Exchange Members, c/o Shearson Lehman International Ltd, Peninsular House, 24 Monument Street, London EC3R 8AJ.

Unlisted Securities Market, The Stock Exchange, Old Broad Street, London EC2N 1HP.

Building Societies

Building Societies Association, 3 Savile Row, London W1X 1AF.

Insurance Market

Association of Lloyds Members, 11 Buckingham Street, London WC2N 6DF.

Lloyds of London, Lime Street, London EC3M 7HA.

Unit Trusts and Investment Trusts

Association of Investment Trust Companies, 6th floor, Park House, 16 Finsbury Circus, London EC2M 7JJ.

Unit Trust Association, 16 Finsbury Square, London EC2M 7JP.

Commodity Markets

Association of Futures Dealers and Brokers, Cereal House, 58 Mark Lane, London EC3R 7NE.

British Federation of Commodity Associations, Plantation House, Mincing Lane, London EC3M 3HT.

International Commodities Clearing House Ltd, Roman Wall House, 1-2 Crutched Friars, London EC3N 2AN.

London Commodity Exchange Co Ltd, Cereal House, 58, Mark Lane, London EC3R 7NE.

Financial Futures Exchange

London International Financial Futures Exchange, Royal Exchange, London EC3A 8E.

Index